MW00834951

On Islam and American Democracy

Commentary of
Imam W. Deen Mohammed

All Rights Reserved

Published by: Ronald B. Shaheed
1101 Lancaster Avenue
Monroe, NC 28112

Sincere thanks and gratitude are extended to Imam/Dr. Nasir Ahmad for his tireless work in digitizing and making available the voluminous lectures and private conversations with Imam W. Deen Mohammed that span 33 years from 1975-2008. We pray that Allah blesses him with good health and long years as he continues this most vital work.

Edited by Ronald B. Shaheed, 2021

ISBN: 978-0-578-93158-6

For other publications on the commentary (tafsir) of Imam W. Deen Mohammed go to: www.thoughtsforsearchers.com

Book cover design by Zuhairah Shaheed

Appreciation for Imam W. Deen Mohammed

"Among the speakers came Imam Wallace D. Muhammed, reciting Qur'anic verses of peace in Arabic and English. An ally of Malcolm X in his youth, Muhammed had gone on to reform his own father's sectarian Nation of Islam. In a book interview, he once had expressed to me his long-term ambition for American Muslims to help reconcile world Islam with democracy. I considered Muhammed the nation's most underappreciated religious figure in the twentieth century, but here he was preaching unnoticed to the incoming Clintons..." *Taylor Branch, (Pulitzer Prize-winning author of "America in the King Years"), "The Clinton Tapes: Wrestling History with the President", Simon & Schuster, New York, NY, 2009, p. 24.*

"The genius of Imam W. D. was that he single-handedly moved the African American community toward identifying with pluralist American identity while moving away from Black Nationalist Islam. Today, millions of African American Muslims are comfortable with being as strongly American as they are being devout Muslims, demonstrating the two are not incompatible. This achievement is due entirely to Imam W. D." *Akbar Ahmed, "Journey into America: The Challenge of Islam", Brookings Institution Press, Washington, D.C., 2010, p. 174.*

"Wallace Deen Muhammed is a dreamer, but he is a dreamer-cum-realist, and gentle, sensitive, and self-effacing. History may yet prove him to be one of the most astute religious leaders of this age, regardless of communion. A lifelong student of Islam, fluent in Arabic, and well conversant with the nuances of Qur'anic ideology and its institutionalized projections, Wallace is no less a keen and perceptive observer of the American scene. Therein lies his potential for achievement and service to Islam." *C. Eric Lincoln, "The Muslim Mission in the Context of American Social History", African-American Religion: Interpretive Essays in History and Culture", T. E. Fulop & A. J. Raboteau, Routledge, New York, NY, 1997, p. 288.*

3

"We have had many meetings with our Muslim friends. What characterizes these gatherings above all is the presence of God which one notices when they pray, and which gives much hope. I saw this hope become a reality in the Malcolm Shabazz Mosque in Harlem (USA) six years ago when I was invited to explain my Christian experience to 3,000 African-American Muslims. Their welcome, beginning with that of their leader, Imam W. D. Mohammed, was so warm, sincere and enthusiastic that it led us to great expectations for the future. I returned three years ago to the United States, to Washington, to make a presentation about our working together before a large convention of 7,000 Christians and Muslims. In an atmosphere of the greatest elation and accompanied by endless applause we exchanged a sincere embrace, promising each other we would continue our journey in the fullest union possible and spread it to others." *Chiara Lubich, leader of the International Focolare Movement, "Chiara Lubich: The Essential Writings", New City Press, Hyde Park, NY, 2007, p. 345.*

"Despite our sharing of existential space with almost 6 billion human beings, in actual fact we know and relate to only a very few of them during our lives. Not so for people like the imam, who grew up as the son of a famous man whose thoughts and actions affected the lives and times of thousands of Americans and others worldwide. Like his father, Warith Deen believed deeply in the capacity and capability of the African American and that their moral and social transformation was imperative. Through words and deeds, he so inspired countless young and old people all over the world that they came to consider him a leader, a mentor, and a friend for life…Although the imam has answered G_d's call, his spirit will continue to affect many of us. He started with what he knew and built on what he had. This was his message, and American students of religious thought and activism will hopefully visit his path and share his findings. Thank G_d Almighty for granting life and good health to this man. He lived well, with love and mercy for all and with dreams and hopes for justice everywhere." *Dr. Sulayman S. Nyang, Howard University, Washington, DC, "The Transformer-in-Chief", Islamic Horizons Magazine, November/December 2008, pp. 16-18.*

Contents

Foreword

Many Muslim Americans, today, are converts from Christianity and many are the harvest of the followers of Imam W. Deen Mohammed's father, the Honorable Elijah Mohammed who led the Nation of Islam from 1933-1975. These same people are the descendants of the victims of the worst system of servitude (slavery) in the history of man. Historian Kenneth M. Stampp said of that system of servitude spawned in America, "Their tragedy did not begin with the ordeal of Reconstruction, or with the agony of civil war, but with the growth of a 'Peculiar institution' (as it is called) in ante-bellum days. It began, in short, with chattel slavery..."[1] In 1835, the Frenchman, Alexis De Tocqueville, wrote: "In one fell swoop, oppression has deprived the descendants of the Africans of almost all the privileges due to human beings! The American Negro has lost even recollection of his homeland; he no longer hears the language of his fathers; he has renounced his religion and forgotten their ways".[2]

The system of chattel slavery to which Stampp and De Tocqueville refer that was imposed upon people forcibly brought from West Africa in the Atlantic slave trade, lasted for nearly 400 years; and is still visited upon the present African American citizens of the United States in the form of a plantation ghost spirit in their souls and psyche. But, ironically, these descendants of Africa that were tried and tested in Mr. Stampp's, "Peculiar institution", in addition to the Jim Crow era of segregation and oppression; the Ku Klux Klan, neo-racism, etc. are, here in the 21st Century, the group of people most prepared to appreciate and represent the best of what American democracy has to offer to the world. Out of this group (African Americans) today, the ones most prepared to lead are the Muslim followers and students of Imam W. Deen Mohammed, because Islam and American democracy have so much in common. In this publication, we have attempted to articulate much of Imam W. Deen Mohammed's commentary on the similarities and differences between Islamic and American democracies. Over his thirty-three years of leadership of Muslims in America Imam W. Deen Mohammed articulated clearly why America is the best nation on earth for the faithful in Islam to live out the guidance in their holy book, the Qur'an, and to follow the life and example of G_d's last Prophet, Muhammed ibn Abdullah of Arabia, peace and blessing be upon him.

We thank Allah for having an opportunity to present such a valuable work as this. May G_d bless America and may G_d bless the world to come to the human destiny outlined by the Prophets in Scripture. We pray that G_d's Peace be upon all of Allah's Prophets and Messengers and upon our noble and honored Prophet, Muhammed; and may G_d bless Imam W. Deen Mohammed to be on the highest plain of the Paradise along with our Prophet.

Ronald B. Shaheed, 2021

Introduction

I was a high school student in the University of Islam, which was really an elementary school and high school, when a person was hired to teach us Arabic. His name was Professor Jamil Diab. He later received his doctorate degree and became, Dr. Jamil Diab. My first acquaintance with him was as his student, one of his students. Dr. Jamil Diab was a very good teacher. He respected the Honorable Elijah Mohammed. He didn't believe as we believed in in the Nation of Islam. He had the belief of Muslims throughout the world and the Honorable Elijah Mohammed knew that when he hired him. But he did not try to make trouble for the Honorable Elijah Mohammed, or for the Nation of Islam. He respected the order of the Nation of Islam and he did the job he was hired for; and that was to teach us the Arabic language.

American Democracy Not Something for Muslims to Fear

Our respect for American democracy began way back there. The point that I'm trying to make, here, is that the form of democracy that we have in America is not something that Muslims have to be afraid of. In fact, it may be closer to what we have as Islamic justice for society than any other political ideology existing in the world, today. Professor Jamil Diab, obviously, recognized that as an immigrant, or as one who migrated from his land to this country and studied this country's government and its idea of democracy. He told us that, "The Constitution of the United States is based upon an idea that Muslims can accept". That's the way he put it to us. He said he had read the introduction to the Constitution, the language of the writers, or the designers of our Constitution, the Founding Fathers, we call them; and Professor Jamil Diab said that he believed that, "They were acquainted with the Qur'an and Muhammed, the Prophet (peace be upon him); those who formed that language".

A Muslim declares his faith by taking shahadatain, saying, "La ilaaha illallah Muhammedar rasulullah". "La ilaaha illallah", is simply translated, "There is no deity, nothing to worship, to pray to as a god, illallah, except the One G_d". That's what it means. Then it says, "Muhammedar rasulullah, Muhammed is the Messenger of G_d." If I believe that declaration of faith, or that statement of the Muslim creed in Islam, it holds in focus for us a concept of G_d and a concept of man; a way of perceiving, or understanding G_d and a way of perceiving and understanding man. And here, G_d and man are put together in one statement: "There is but the One G_d and Muhammed is the Messenger of G_d". In one statement the two are put together.

A Man Like Moses

Muhammed did not come to just invite people to a spiritual way of life. He came to establish a spiritual way of life as the essential life of community. So, the interest was to strengthen community and Muhammed is unlike many of the Prophets, especially, minor Prophets of the Bible. Muhammed was a Prophet, like Moses, and he's called that in our religion and in the Qur'an, *"A man like Moses"*. Prophet Muhammed and Prophet Moses were very similar in that both of them came to lead their people into community life.[3]

The Jews were oppressed. They were a subject people, or an underclass people, under Pharaoh's Egypt, under ancient Egypt, oppressive Egypt, because Egypt was not always oppressive. Egypt did not always have a hard taskmaster. When we study the history of Egypt, many of the Pharaohs were very kind to their public, to their citizens and they believed in strengthening the social family, the fabric of the society; and some of them even guided their publics to the belief that there was but One G_d.

The Life for the Betterment of Society

I am not here to give you that history, so, I won't give you a lot of notes, or information on that; although I know it. I studied it and I do know it. It's simply to say that Muhammed, the Prophet, was guided by G_d to establish spiritual life as the life for the betterment of society so that society could exist and have a good future, and progress in the line of progress that G_d, the Creator, intended for them.

And this is the language of the Founding Fathers: "We hold these truths to be self-evident, that all men are created equal and endowed by their Creator..." Here is the language of the Founding Fathers, recognizing G_d, recognizing the Creator, and recognizing all men as having unalienable rights that the government can't give to them. You were created with those rights, unalienable rights, among these, life, liberty and the pursuit of happiness.

True Democracy Recognizes Higher Authority Than Man

In my studies, I have come to see such statements, that statement, as a statement of strong faith and allegiance to G_d. So, the writers of this language, they were building an idea that would tie man to G_d and would insist, or force government to recognize that tie between man and G_d; a tie that government didn't make; a tie that government cannot break. Government has to recognize that tie and treat all citizens as the creation of G_d and that G_d gave them certain rights that man, or the world, or the government cannot take away from them.

This is the beauty of, I would say, that idea and this is what makes for a true democracy. A true democracy must recognize that there is an Authority higher than man. That is a true democracy that recognizes that there is an Authority higher than man and people are accountable to their Maker; people are accountable to their Creator, the One that designed their life and gave them life.

Religions Co-exist That Recognize G_d as Creator

And this life that we have is a very precious life. So, we perceive G_d as the Creator of everything; yet, G_d did not tell Muhammed, when He first gave him revelation that, "I am Allah." Prophet Muhammed, later, came to know the name, Allah (Highly Gloried is He). It was not in the first revelation to Muhammed. G_d introduced Himself to Muhammed, firstly, as the Creator; not by the name, Allah, but as the Creator. And every religion that recognizes G_d as the One Who is responsible for what we see in the skies, for the earth that we live on; and whatever comes out of the earth, and for man's own existence; those religions that recognize G_d as that, those religions can live together. They can co-exist together. Those religions can do more than co-exist together. Those religions can work together and cooperate with one another for the future of mankind, because that is the precious idea that makes it possible for us to make progress with our human life in society.

That's the precious idea, that there is a Maker, there is a Designer; that this did not happen, accidentally. There is a Designer for what is in the skies, for what we see in the sky; this system of matter with stars, etc. There is a Designer behind that and it is the same Designer, that is, also, the Cause for our human existence. And just as that Designer has designed the course for matter in the skies, that Designer has designed the course for man's life, for human life on earth and it must be lived in community.

Human Beings Created to Follow Definite Patterns

The expression, *"Thy Kingdom come, Thy Will be done on earth as it is in heaven"*,[4] is another way of saying that G_d has ordered the universe and brought it to exist in a certain order and design, and has preserved it with that design. That, also, says the sun must keep going the way it goes. The moon must keep going the way it goes, and the stars must keep following the courses they follow, etc.

The Qur'an, our holy book, and the Bible, address that. Both of our holy books, the book of Christians and the book of Muslims, address that. So, the same G_d that has designed that has, also, created and designed human life to follow laws, to follow definite patterns of behavior, definite patterns of discipline, or behavior, so that the life will continue and make progress.

"Thy Kingdom come, Thy Will be done, on earth, as it is in heaven." So, these people were visionaries. These people were deep thinkers, philosophers, who believed in G_d. They had a spiritual devotion to a G_d, to the Creator and they were working to have man's life conform to the universal law. The same G_d that made that up there made this down here. And as He made an order and a plan for that up there, we have to discover the order and plan that He made for this down here. That's what it was all about.

Contributing to the Lifeline of American Society

So, America recognizes that. The government recognizes that. That is the strength of our Constitution. That is the strongest glue, or adhesive matter holding together the idea we call, Western democracy. So, when we appreciate this, as Muslims and identify that language with our language, or our language with that language, we are in a good situation to make progress in this society; to make progress, not just for our publics; but to make progress for our leaders. No Muslim should be satisfied just being a member in another public. Muslims should, also, be contributing to the lifeline of the society that they are in. They should identify its lifeline and they should join the guardians of that lifeline and make contributions to that lifeline for the better future for all.

This is where Muslims should be. We still are talking about democracy. I know some Muslims appreciate it and some are so afraid of it that they are, "Spooked up". I'm telling you the boogieman has some of them. But, Allah willing, we will get the boogieman out of our life, one day, and we want our Christian friends to know how we see America, how we see the idea that preserves this country and the way of life of the American people.

One Day Muhammed and Jesus Together

We want them to know that we are not that far away from them. In fact, we should not be apart from each other at all. We should be together. Muhammed, the Prophet, said, "One day, the world will see Jesus Christ and me together." He did not say that just as breath in the air. He said that as a prediction. That statement is, also, a prediction that Christians and Muslims are going to come closer and closer together. If the world comes to see Muhammed and Jesus Christ as closer and closer together, then the Christians will appreciate Islam when they see that their Christ and Muhammed, the Prophet, are close together. It means that the two communities are going to come closer together because of those two figures being seen close together; and it is happening now in the world and it is growing.

Islam Restored Man and Freedom of Religion

Islam is an idea, or an ideology that G_d has revealed, or given to man to reform the world; and it did it. Yes, Islam came to free not only man's human life, but it came to free religion that had lost its good guardians and had fallen into the hands of oppressors. And oppressors were reinterpreting religion, restating religion all over, again, to satisfy their design, or their desire to have the human being under their control. Religion was used to oppress and enslave people. It fell into the hands of the wrong leaders, the wrong powers, and Islam came and addressed that.

Muhammed was told by G_d (in the Qur'an), *"And fight them until there is no more persecution of the sincere, true believers, and religion is free for G_d".*[5] It didn't say, "Islam". It said, "Religion". We know it means Islam, but it said religion. It was, also, for the Church. It was, also, for Christianity. It was, also, for Judaism. It was, also, for the Synagogue. It was for the Jews that Muhammed was fighting oppressors, the persecutors of the faithful. It said, *"Fight them, until there is no more persecution and religion is free for G_d".* Do you hear that? These words are from our holy book, the Qur'an.

Islam Came to Promote Freedom of Religion

Now tell me, if you understand the simple English that I just gave you, did Islam come to promote freedom of religion, or not? That statement is very clear. You need no explanation, or interpretation of that. It says, *"Fight them, until there is no more persecution..."* of the religious people, the faithful people who insist that, "I must follow G_d, the way G_d intends for me to follow and you government people, you'll have to kill me! I will not give up my faith, or my obedience to my G_d!" And they would kill you! Many of the faithful died. We know that Christians, Muslims, Jews, and many of the faithful died and are still dying in many parts of the world for their religion.

Islam came to promote freedom of religion and freedom of religion is the first of our freedoms. This is the United States government's political idea. When you study it you will find, in the history of our political idea for democracy, that it begins with the freedom of religion. First, there was the fight for the freedom of religion; then there was the fight for all the other freedoms. The Pilgrims came over here because they were persecuted and could not practice their religion, in Europe, like they wanted to. So, they found that there was a new land over here, and they were invited to come here to see if they could start their lives, again.

Democracy Begins with Freedom of Religion

They came here to see if they could start their lives, again, so that they would have the opportunity to live their Christianity, or their church life, as they wanted to live it without having that denied to them by the powers in their old land; by governments, in their old land. This is the beginning of freedom, here. So, this democracy began with the first freedom, the freedom of religion. Islam, too, begins with the first freedom, the freedom of religion. When Muhammed gave the creed, "There is no god but Allah and Muhammed is the Messenger of Allah", he was making a statement in the defense of the freedom of religion.

In our religion, Islam, we are told: *"Surely, the idea that there is more than One G_d is the worst of the oppressors, or the worst form of oppression"*;[6] the idea that there is more than one G_d. The pagans, the people in Mecca, in Arabia, in the time of our Prophet, they believed in 369 deities. This is the history. They had 369 different deities, different gods, and they were an ignorant and oppressed people. They were in the darkness. What darkness? The darkness of the absence of light on the path that takes man and society where G_d wants man and society to go. That's the darkness.

"Making His Way Home to Me"

So, G_d created not only the individual for a higher life, but G_d created communities of human beings for a higher life. And the greatest ideas for advancing society, or government, are those ideas that have the support of revelation, Scripture (Bible, Qur'an, etc.); so that the leaders, when they become enlightened in that particular knowledge, they then can take the society forward to where G_d wants it to go. And where does G_d want it to go? *"I am what I shall be. I shall be what I am."*[7] What does that mean? It means, "I

15

recognize that G_d has created me with that that will place me where I should be in the future. I have to discover it. G_d has created me with it, but I have to discover it. When I discover what G_d has endowed me with, when I discover what G_d has enriched me with as a special creation of His, I will discover what will put me where I am to go. I may be a lost savage eating with animals and living like an animal; but when I wake up to what G_d has made me I will separate myself from the animals. I will separate myself from the savages, and I will pursue the course that G_d has designed for me when He designed me. I will be what I am, and I am, already, what I shall be". But it has to be discovered and G_d sees man struggling to find himself and G_d looks at him and says, "Oh, My creation is wonderful! My creation is beautiful! I gave him nothing more than I gave the animals. But on his own, on the power of what I created him to be, he is struggling and making his way Home to Me."

G_d then says, "It is time for Me, now, to go out and meet My creation." G_d then gives him revelation from Himself, and G_d says, *"Yes, I am the One Who created you from a clot of adhering blood"*.[8] Then G_d reveals to him his destination, where he is to take his life and the life of his fellow man. He then becomes a Prophet, a leader, a liberator, and a builder of a great society. Moses did it. Muhammed did it and others did it.

Slavery Cut Off the Spirit and Lifeline of G_d

I can't, myself, discuss Islam without, also, discussing the African American people's life and struggle to put ourselves back in that place of honor that G_d created us for. Slavery separated us from that life pattern, from that lifeline. It cut us off from that spirit and lifeline that G_d created us with and for. But our souls were created by G_d and the world could not deceive our souls. They deprived our minds of knowledge and guidance, but they couldn't deceive our souls. So, the soul of the uneducated slave spoke out to the master. The name of this soul was, Julia, in history. The slave, Julia, she spoke to her white master. Speaking to all of them, she said, "You all look like G_d in the face", because they had told her Jesus was G_d and they did look like Jesus in the face. She said, "You look like G_d, in the face, but you act like the devil in your hearts!"

Now, that was an uneducated slave woman that had some trouble inside accepting that that white world was all right. So, they could deceive the mind of the slave, but they could not deceive the soul; because that's the sacred vessel that G_d made and they cannot take it away from us. You can't even take it away from yourself. I don't care how much corruption you allow to take over in your life, your soul will, occasionally, let you know, "You are wrong!" G_d created the soul and it has a sentry in it. You can blind the outer perimeters of the soul. You can have the soul supporting your corruption in its outer perimeters; but every now and then, it speaks from its core, out of the core that you can't touch. It is the sanctuary of G_d that you can't touch. It will say to you that you ought to clean up your act.

Return to What G_d Created You With

We can't talk about Islam without talking about our lives. Muhammed, the Prophet was never sent to human beings to talk about Islam without talking about their lives. He addressed human life and G_d educated him to address the problems of human life, so the human being would see that what G_d wants for you is to have the excellence of your life; for you to rise up from the inferior matter of your life and build yourself up on the superior matter of your life. And what is the superior matter of your life? It is that inherent dignity. G_d says, *"We have certainly made honorable every human being born of your father, Adam",* our common father.[9]

And that honor, or G_d-given nobility, is never pleased to be reduced to dishonor. It always wants to live up to what G_d created it to be. Therefore, human beings are, by virtue of their creation, or their original nature given to them by G_d, motivated to make improvement on their lives; motivated and inspired to make improvements on their life until they reach that honor that G_d created them for.

From Europe to America, those who paid a heavy price to have freedom of religion paved the way for the development of this democracy and for the freedoms that we now enjoy in America and Europe and in many places of the world. So, they are the ones that made possible this society that we have in the New World. Patrick Henry said, "Give me liberty, or give me death!" Thomas Paine wrote a pamphlet, *Common Sense*. These men were great factors in the creation of this great society. They saw the need to leave those who were in the ivory towers, those with the great ideas, with academic knowledge and ask the society to return to common sense. And what does it mean? It means return to what G_d created you with.

"Give Us Death or Give Us Life!"

That's another testimony to what I am saying, here. It supports my point. Patrick Henry said, "Give me liberty, or give death". Now, here is a man that when he's saying that, he is asking people to follow him. That's what he's doing. He's asking people, the society to, "Follow me. Let's tell these oppressors that we would rather have death than to live without the life that G_d intended for us. Give me life, or give me death". Give me the life that G_d created for me, or, give me death". Well, a great man, long before Patrick Henry, he put it this way. They were about to go to battle with the people that was persecuting them, and he sent a message to the persecutors that told them, "Before we begin the battle, we want you to know that we have fighters over here with us that love death more than you love life. Now, let's get it on!" They were defeated. Right then, that defeated them. Those warriors heard that yelled out to them in their ears. They said, "Before we get the battle on now, we want you to know that we have fighters over here who love death like you love life".

What were they saying? They were saying, "Give us death, or give us life!" They were saying the same thing that Patrick Henry said, just a different way of stating it. Patrick Henry, he stated it, differently, but it's the same thing, meaning that, "We will not continue to live under persecution and suffer the denial of the life that G_d created us for. We'd rather die, if this is the way we're going to live". That's what Patrick Henry was saying and that's what Prophet Muhammed was saying when he was taking his men into war, or into battle against those who persecuted them.

First Reform in the Church

Martin Luther, the great church reform leader, he helped paved the way for our democracy. None of this could exist without these great leaders I am mentioning. We couldn't have this great society, if it had not been for them. The first reform, then, had to take place in the Church. Then after the reform in the Church, we had the political movement for this great society, or for this great democracy.

Now, getting back to Islam, the first understanding that I had of the word, "Islam", was, "Islam is freedom, justice and equality". That meaning lives, today, in the hearts and minds of many of us whose first acquaintance with Muslims and Islam began in the city of Detroit, the Motor City, with the Honorable Elijah Mohammed and his teacher, Mr. W. Fard Muhammad. And I recall words being painted on the blackboard. I was a boy and I would be sitting in my seat in the Temple, with the men and with the children, sometimes, too, and there was a blackboard there with paint on it. And the blackboard said, "Islam is Freedom, Justice and Equality." We could see it as soon as we entered the seating area where the lecture, or preaching, would be done. As soon as you got in that area, the first thing to hit your eyes was that blackboard, with Islam as the staff and, "Freedom, Justice and Equality", going out from, the word, Islam.

Today, learned Muslim authors of Islamic publications are discussing Islam as a universal message for promoting human progress, social and economic justice, etc. One such publication is titled, *The Minaret of Freedom*. I became acquainted with them several years, or more ago. I was so happy to see educated Muslims in America embracing the idea of freedom and calling Muslims' attention to the great idea of freedom.

Some Muslim Leaders Fear Being Seen as Friends of the West

However, some leaders in Islam, sometimes, fear to use the language that the West uses when that language is really their own language. But they fear to use it because they are afraid that using it will cause them to be seen as friends of the West. Isn't that a bad situation to be in? You can't even speak your own language for fear that someone is going to think you are the friend of your enemy. That is ridiculous! Why won't you be a friend to those who think like you? Why won't you be their friend? Why won't you be a friend of those who want what you want and then join them and they will help you fight their own people who are against that? You see, Allah, G_d, the Creator of all of us, He will never help us if we are selfish and not standing upon truth and justice. If we are standing upon hurt and bitterness, He is not going to help us, if we are not standing on truth and justice at the same time.

It is okay. You are supposed to register and you are supposed to dislike hurt. But you are not supposed to stand upon hurt. "Oh, my position is that you did me wrong!" No, my position is that wrong is wrong, whether done to me, or anybody else. So, I am standing on the principle, not on the pain, not on the hurt to me. I am standing on the principle. A man can fight much longer fighting for principles than he can fighting for hurt. After a while, you are not hurting so much and you'll stop fighting. But there is a need to continue to fight for the principle because there are others, hurting. Now, here is the difference between what Islam wants for society and what America wants for society. In principle, America and Islam want the same thing for man; in principle. But in practice, they are different. America seems to put the emphasis and light on freedom more so than on justice.

Islam Sometimes Sacrifices Freedom for Justice

And the result is that the society is turned on to freedom, but not, necessarily, turned on to justice. My freedom may disrespect your freedom and my freedom may clash with your freedom. So, the society suffers because we are going after freedom, but have lost the connection for freedom with justice. Freedom and justice are born together and freedom and justice are to live together, always. You are to never to separate justice from freedom. In Islam, justice is willing to sacrifice some freedom for freedom, or for a genuine freedom down the road. But freedom, in Islam, is never willing to sacrifice any part of justice. It is not justice that you punish the victims to recover from the wrong, or the injuries of the guilty. I know some of you are following what I'm saying. That's why in Islam, we say, *"No bearer of a burden should bear the burden of another"*.[10]

Chapter 1

Strengthening Our American Citizenship

If people love you, you have to love them and their love for you makes you want to know them better, too; because you think about them more. And, really, when you're good, you are fit for anybody's religion. A good person is fit for anybody's religion. So, you have to embrace them just like you embrace one another; forming alliances so that we will have more opportunity to grow, financially, and to build loyalty. Now, what is our first loyalty? What is the first tie, or bond, for loyalty? It is G_d. The number one obligation for our loyalty is to G_d. We have to be loyal to G_d, first, above this country and this is nothing that you should be afraid to listen to. This is nothing that you should be afraid to shout out, that your loyalty is not to your country, first! Your loyalty is to G_d, first! The reason why our citizenry has become so terrible, so funky, so rotten, is because our loyalty is not to G_d, first. Loyalty should be to G_d, first, then to your country. Countrymen used to have the loyalty of savages, the loyalty of gangsters. This is the history of the world. That's the loyalty they used to have, the loyalty of savages and gangsters.

Governments Formed Better After Revelation Came

You have heard about loyalty among thieves, or honor among thieves, etc. That's the kind of loyalty there was until revelation came to them from G_d and it lifted their minds up high in the stratosphere of purity, sincerity, and truthfulness. It lifted their minds up so high that they then were able to formulate a picture, or a concept of how man's life is to be governed on this earth. As a result, new and better governments began to be created. Find me a government that has survived without the people of that government claiming that higher idea, or claiming that a higher interest than man in his mortal form has to come, or has to be realized by them.

Find me the most advanced government on earth in terms of what man needs to survive and prosper; especially, in a world that's going to be more and more populated, more and more difficult to live in with others; others that you don't even like, sometimes. Find me some nations, other than those nations who claim Scripture, their people claim Scripture, that are in the lead in this world. Christians are in the lead. Jews are in the lead. Muslims are in the lead, ahead of everybody else. Even the Hindu and the Buddhist, although they have, too, an inspired life, their life, too, is inspired by visionaries and seers that claim a dimension, a reality, above the mortal life. So, they, also, have a claim on a dimension that's above the mortal life. I mean the human in his flesh and blood life. They are the ones that are leading the world. Shouldn't that be evidence to us that if you want to be really successful on the earth, in a political and material environment, you had better connect onto what those people have connected to; a belief in a higher reality, superior to man's capacity and abilities to manage for himself?

Belief in the Unseen

The extra help comes to man, the human being, only when he's able to connect with the unknown, "Bil ghaib". "Bil ghaib", means belief in Allah (G_d) without help from your eyes. It means it's absent from my eyes. I can't see it with my eyes. It comes from the word, "Absent", but it says, *"Belief in the Unseen"*. That's the translation.[11] But, actually, what it means is it is absent from my grasp. I cannot grasp it with my eyes and my intelligence; not even with my intelligence can I fully grasp it. But I yet believe in it because, as the Scripture says, *"Well, I know he opened my blinded eyes. That's good enough for me"*. There was a person who had been blessed by Jesus Christ to have their sight come back to them and they were questioned about him. They said, "Well, I believe in him. The only thing I know is that he gave me sight and I had no sight. He gave my sight back to me".

Build Your Future with Respect for G_d First

Well, there are many people like me. I'm a witness, myself, that I was blind and G_d gave me sight. G_d opened my eyes and I don't know how He did it. Allah says in Qur'an of Jesus Christ when he would be asked about the charges that he made himself a god with G_d, he would say, *"G_d, you know what is in myself, but I know not what is in Yourself"*.[12] It means, G_d is the Unknown. To even the closest person to G_d, G_d is still a mystery. G_d is never fully grasped by any human being, or anything other than G_d. G_d is known only by Himself, in totality. We can only know Him in part and we should know this. This makes for a better change of life on this planet earth, when you accept that and begin to build your future with respect for G_d, firstly, and then your nation, secondly. How can we improve upon the nation if we don't have an eraser bigger than the nation's eraser? The nation has got an eraser and can't clean the board. We need an eraser bigger than the United States.

A Script Bigger Than the Constitution of the United States

G_d gives us an eraser in the Qur'an. It's bigger than the United States' eraser. We can clean the board when we want to. And then, He gives us a script bigger than the Constitution of the United States. We can, also, write for the United States, one day. Why not? Others are doing it and the Founding Fathers made this provision that, "We have done our best, but in the future, if this doesn't work, you have authorization from us", to do what? Change it! Get rid of it! I read it. Perhaps, you didn't read it well enough. Perhaps, you didn't read it good enough. It didn't say, "You only have the authorization to change it." It says, "You have the authorization to get rid of it and bring in a new one". The Founding Fathers didn't say, "Oh, this is for G_d, don't touch it!" They said, "This is for man; man, trusting in G_d, doing his best. But if, one day, it should fail you, you have the authorization from us to change it, or, abolish it and bring in a new one".

World Changed Because Persons Believed

We need to build respect more than we need to build courage. But we, also, need to build courage when it comes to changing the world. We think, "The world, we can't change it." Look, if the world could not be changed, African Americans would still be on the plantation as slaves. Somebody believed that the world could be changed. That is why we are not on the plantation as slaves. For African Americans, the Honorable Elijah Mohammed came and G_d inspired him to be a leader to make us come out of the fear to do the things we know we should do to make our life better.

Muhammed, the Prophet, Bigger Than Political Leaders

He came to take us out of that fear, so we would have the courage and the boldness to take our lives into our own hands and do what we know we should do with it. Therefore, should we be worshipers of the United States and worshipers of the laws, or the Constitution of these United States above our respect for G_d, the Qur'an, and the teachings and life of Muhammed, the Prophet? He (Muhammed, the Prophet) is bigger than all the political leaders in the universe.

If there could be someone on the planet, Mars, I'm including them, too. Muhammed, the Prophet, is bigger than all the political leaders that exist anywhere on earth, or anywhere. He's bigger than them because G_d spoke to him. You either believe it, or you don't. G_d spoke to him. He got directions, directly, from the Creator of the heavens and the earth; the One Who made man when man was not existing.

We Need to Have a Strategy

The Qur'an says, *"Who knows best, the one who was born, or the One that's been in existence, always, and never changes?"* That's G_d. That's Allah, highly glorified is He. We need to build loyalty, first, with Allah. Our loyalty is, first, to our G_d Who created us and that's the way you should know G_d. Know G_d, firstly, as your Creator, the One that made possible your existence, and the existence of everything. That's first. You say, "Oh, well, we should know Allah, Ar Rahmaan (the Merciful Benefactor), Ar Raheem (the Merciful Redeemer) because every chapter of Qur'an opens up with, 'Bismillah Ar Rahmaan, Ar Raheem' (With G_d's Name, the Merciful Benefactor, the Merciful Redeemer)." But when G_d spoke to Muhammed, He didn't say, "Bismillah Ar Rahmaan, Ar Raheem". He said, *"Read in the name of your Lord Who Created"*.[13] He introduced Himself as the Creator, not as Ar Rahmaan, Ar Raheem. Building loyalty needs a strategy. G_d gives us the strategy for building loyalty with Him, or to Him; but we need, also, a strategy for building loyalty wherever we want to build that loyalty; with others of our circumstances; with good people, who are in the good human condition, like we have for ourselves; or like we want for ourselves, etc. We need to have a strategy. Our religion gives us the preparation for everything good. If we want to have loyalty with other people, the strategy we need, believe me, the preparation for having that loyalty, is given in Qur'an and Muhammed, the Prophet's life.

No Value as Citizens

All of us are citizens of the United States, but don't think that our citizenship is of the same quality, or of the same value. Some, because of their ignorance, their citizenship is very cheap; and other citizens who are conscious citizens, see how they live? But, they don't value those citizens at all. So, because of their ignorance, they are citizens of America, but they have no value. They have no value for us, or for good Americans. They have no value, those who stay in jail all the time and commit crimes. As soon as they are out on the street for a little while, they commit more crime and they are back in jail. What value do they have as citizens for this country? They are nothing but a burden on the citizens of this country. They burden all of us. They hurt our life. They cause us material loss and then, when they lock them up, they take our money to take care of them while they're locked up. They're of no value to us, as citizens. We wish they weren't existing. I know that when I say this it makes some of us flinch. You would be flinching a lot if I were in power.

The Need to Strengthen Our American Citizenship

We need to strengthen our American citizenship. And if we want to strengthen our American citizenship we should, first of all, take the first position as a citizen of America and that is that we are citizens of America. We're citizens of the United States of America. Our flag is the Star-spangled Banner. That's what our flag is, the American flag and we show respect for it to let you know that you're wasting your time if you think we're backing up off of it! This is not just sentimentalism, or emotionalism. This is wisdom and this is truthfulness. Be truthful. We're citizens of the United States of America and because of our citizenship, we have the conditions for our life, here, that we have.

This country has greatly improved over the last hundred years, or so. It has greatly improved for us (African Americans). Now, if we were going to leave, shouldn't we have left when it was bad for us? If we are going to put thumbs down on America, the President, and everybody leading the country, shouldn't we have done that when it was bad for us? As soon as it becomes nice for us and they are willing to sacrifice their lives to have people to respect our equal rights, with them, as citizens, shouldn't we show that we appreciate that? Shouldn't we show by our own actions that we realize that this is a changed time? Don't let our actions say, "Nothing has changed! They don't like us". Believe me, if you take that attitude, even those that you think may like you, they're planning for you. They've got a plan to eliminate you. Yes, indeed! They're watching you and they are not sensible, intelligent, human beings, if they are not watching you. Here you are in this country, sharing citizenship and the benefits of the law with them, and they are going to let you go against the interest of the country and not watch you? They are going to watch you.

I remember, once, the FBI was questioning me and I was happy to be questioned because I wanted to talk to the FBI. I was outside of the Nation of Islam. They put me out. I wanted to tell the FBI that, "I don't believe my father is responsible for the stuff that you're hearing about and that you're coming to me about; i.e., a black mafia, operating in Philadelphia, operating in Kansas City, operating in Detroit". So, they come to me with this stuff and they were asking me questions. I was happy they came to me because I wanted to tell them, "I know my father. I'm his son. I know him, personally". I said, "No, this is not him. This is not my father". And they said, "We didn't think it was". They were happy to get my reply. They said, "Well, you're telling us what we thought." They said, "Wallace" They call you by your first name. They've got their psychology. If they say to you, "Are you Wallace D. Mohammed?" that's the only time they are going to mention your last name. "Well, Wallace, don't you think you ought to go back to your father?" I said, "I didn't put myself out. I can't go back." They wanted me back and that was good.

That told me they wanted good people to be the leader because I was a good man. I know that. I've never been a bad man. They wanted me back to be near my father, so, if something happened I would be there to help my father. I would be in position, maybe, to be the next leader. They didn't say that, but I'm sure that was their thinking. So, I liked that from them. I liked knowing that from them.

Strong and Healthy People of Substance

In building loyalty, we have to improve upon our citizenship. Our citizenship becomes much more observable and much more appreciated by the strong and healthy people of substance and value when they know that we are like them, identifying with the country in its best nature and in its best developments. I'm not identifying with the Ku Klux Klan. There is a lot of stuff, here in America, that we know we're against. But Americans didn't live to have the Klan exist. Americans lived to have freedom reign for all.

These ugly things, you have to see them as things that have been imposed upon the America, or the United States envisioned by the Founding Fathers. These things have been imposed upon America and the good citizens have been working to get rid of these ugly things and have met with a lot of success. So, let's realize the new time and identify with true Americans against those who just get benefits, while making life hard for others.

Let us identify with the real, serious and true Americans, not with crazy fanatics, who have their idea of America and they want to impose that narrow, small idea on others. No, we have the Founding Fathers' idea of America and that's the idea that includes all of us and recognizes G_d, the Creator, above the country. I don't think we could have a better situation, unless it was the same in its construction, but under the Qur'an and under Muhammed's leadership and his model. That's the only way it could be better.

The Freedom of America is Our Freedom

It would have to have the same construction, the same protection for the rights of everybody; free market and free enterprise. Did Muhammed come and try to regulate business? No, he didn't. He trusted business people to establish business and to be responsible for business. So, didn't we have free enterprise before America? Certainly, we did. So, don't say, "Oh, this is un-Islamic, brother, embracing this free enterprise". You can't even embrace American freedom without some so-called Muslim authority telling you, "This is un-Islamic. That's not ours. This democracy and freedom here, brother, is not ours". Well, it's not ours, up to a point. But in the vision of the Founding Fathers the freedom of America is our freedom, too.

America's Freedom Not for Perversion

The Founding Fathers didn't envision any freedom for you to be a gangster, or freedom for you to be unfair to others. There was no freedom for you to become a pervert, for you to sell pornography, or for you to engage in pornography and corrupt the lives of little children and teenagers. The Founding Fathers, they would have gone to war to stop such things. So, our idea of freedom is the idea of freedom that is formal and authorized by the Founding Fathers. It's part of the document we call, the Constitution of the United States. That's our concept of freedom, not the freedom to go out there and set up gambling joints, etc.; go to Las Vegas to get rich; the freedom to have prostitutes. All of this that exists of freedom to go outside of the context of the Founding Fathers, there are laws set up against such. When an immigrant comes here, he becomes so emotional and reactive that often, he's prone to react without thinking, without the history of this land. He can't have that knowledge if he's just prejudiced and given to jump to conclusions.

It Takes Patience to Know the Beauty of America

It takes patience to know the beauty of America. There is trouble in any people's history. Trouble can occupy the mind and take the attention. Look for life that belongs to the original, what was the original, what was the pattern. It takes patience to see what developed in the line of time. You have to have patience. We can't expect this kind of protection for our citizens to come, if they come with their own flag in their briefcase and they're still in Pakistan, Malaysia, etc.; if so, we've got aliens who raised their right hands and told a lie. Let me make this very clear. I'm a Muslim leader for all Muslims. I know that most of the Muslims are good. Most Pakistani, Egyptians, name any group, most are good. Most Libyans are good.

During slavery, there were a few who wanted to decide life for African Americans. They were not with the majority. The majority never accepted our enslavement. They couldn't have slaves in the North; not to say they didn't benefit from it. They didn't turn heads away. At least, we know they were not the ones that wanted that. The great sinners and oppressors were not the majority. So, it is for the majority of Muslims in the world. Consequently, the interest of the international ummah (community of Muslims) is my interest and I won't be happy here, until we have better conditions for all Muslims.

Home to Ourselves

Allah never said the Ka'bah (the house that is the orientation for Muslims' prayer) was for Muslims, only. It was built for all people.[14] We identify, firstly, with roots not as Muslims, but as humans that, firstly, identity with Islam; then, G_d revealed to us the nature to obey Him, to put our will below His; then He called us, "Muslims". We put our will under the Will of G_d. G_d's Purpose for us is above us. Islam has its roots in nature before it has roots in history. I am emphasizing this so our faith will be strengthened by increased knowledge and insight. If we are faithful, we will make correct choices; clearer, honorable, stronger, and more lasting choices; and build loyalty for G_d and Islam as citizens, as Americans. That brings us home to ourselves.

A Mercy to All Creatures

The Qur'an was revealed to Prophet Muhammed of Arabia, who was a native-born child of Mecca, persecuted by his own people for no other reason than he said, "Your G_d is One G_d". He had to leave the city of his birth and go to Madinah where there was an indication from the citizens of that city to come and teach the religion that G_d had ordered him to give to all mankind. We are the followers of that man and G_d says of him, *"He is a flesh and blood person, just like yourselves"*.[15] He did not claim to be an angel. He claimed no divinity. G_d loved him as His creation and chose him and made him a mercy to all people. It is told to us in the Qur'an that he is a mercy to all the worlds.

Religion's Purpose to Transform Humanity

If we are his followers, then we should be like him. We should, also, be a mercy to all the worlds. The House (Ka'bah) that we look to for direction in prayer and, also, for Hajj, Pilgrimage, to perform the sacred rites of the Pilgrimage, G_d says of that house, *"It is a house built for all mankind"*. And G_d does not address mankind as Arabs, or as a particular nation. G_d addresses mankind as one. G_d says many times in the Qur'an, *"Oh, mankind!"*. What is Islam's universal message? As Maulana Maududi of Pakistan, the late Islamic reformer of Pakistan said, "It is an idea for the transformation of the whole world". And that's what religion comes for. Religion comes to transform life, transform society, so that the society will come from purposeless life, or interest, to purposeful life; and to the whole interest that G_d created the human being for. And that interest, we know, in Islam and we know, also, from readings in the other great religions, that that interest is that the human being benefits, fully, from the world that G_d created.

Islam Promotes Healthy Citizenship

So, Islam supports and promotes good citizenship, healthy citizenship; and the way it does this is very easy to explain. It only takes a very few words, although, I will give the topic more time. We know that what makes the society, the city, or town bad for us is the people who are bad. Without bad people, towns are good. So, the simple answer to how Islam promotes healthy citizenship is by promoting healthy-minded persons, citizens.

Christianity, says, as I read in the Bible, *"As a man thinks in his heart, so is he"*.[16] It didn't say, "Thinks in his head". It says, "Thinks in his heart." It connects the heart with the thinking. This is what Islam wants for us, too, that we reflect on things. When I was a child in school, one thing they told me was that I would have to learn a lot of things by heart. One thing the school encouraged us to do was to learn a lot by memory, although they said, "Learn it by heart."

Learn It by Heart

That expression means, "To make that learning very, very special and give it your concern, to value it and care about it." I was talking to someone, who kept forgetting things that we were trying to remember. I said, "The reason you can't remember it is that you don't care enough about it. If you care enough about it, you will remember it. Learn it by heart." It has to be in the heart, too, not just in the mind. And when the heart and mind are working together, then you can get the best benefit from your brain, or mind. But if they are not working together, then you won't get the best benefit from your brain. This is how Islam promotes healthy citizenship. Islam wants us to reflect, and reflect means to do more than just think about it. It means to think about what it is worth to you and what you want it for. Think about what you are going to do with it. Think. Think. Think. Think. Think with the heart involved.

I tend to be a bit philosophical, and once, I was told this and it made me angry, because I wasn't thinking about philosophy. I was just trying to get my points across and a very learned person and great Islamic scholar, with a great reputation, from Egypt, originally, he said to me after I finished, "Your statements are more philosophy than religion." His comments angered me, because I didn't think it was philosophy. I thought it was just common sense, because I tend to think in pictures and speak through pictures.

"By the Fig and the Olive and Mt. Sinai"

There is a saying in the Qur'an, the holy book of Muslims. It is for all people, just like the Bible is for all people. The Qur'an says, *"By the Fig and the Olive and Mt. Sinai and this town made safe, secured, surely, We have created the human being in the best of molds"*.[17] There was a time when there were no public schools. Public schools came late in the history of nations where you have to send your children to school; and if you don't, you are subject to be put in jail, taken to court, and locked up for not permitting your children to get an education. So, now education is enforced for the society.

I believe that the reference I just gave from our holy book has in it the importance of education. It is addressing the stages in the mind, the intellect; the stages of how the mind develops. The first is given in a picture, and that is the way I used to talk (with pictures). When I preached years ago, they called me, "Minister Wallace". I was a young man. I wasn't a leader then. I was just a preacher for my father. And they would say, "Brother Minister, you paint beautiful pictures." I liked it, but it did not register too much on my mind, then. But when I look back, now, I see that I need a picture to start talking.

I see the reference to the fig in this verse in the Qur'an and when you think about the fig, the Qur'an doesn't give any commentary on it. It leaves the commentary for the scholars. It leaves the commentary for the thinkers. When you think about the fig, it is bigger than the olive and it has many seeds; whereas, the olive has just one seed. So, it goes from a product, or a fruit that is easy to chew. You don't have to worry about a fig. Even if it is dry, you don't have to worry about it. If you bite an olive and don't have any caution, you are going to break your dentals. Even a young person might hurt their teeth, if they bite down on that stone inside. It is hard. It is not like the fig that you can chew through. The olive has only one seed, but you must be careful eating it. You can't rush and eat it like you do the fig. The fig has many seeds and it's like a burst of seeds; and think about the expression, "That's a figment of your imagination."

Make the Town Safe by Respecting All People

The olive is in the Bible and it is, also, in the Qur'an. The Qur'an mentions the fig, first. The fig is kind of put down in the Bible. But here, the Qur'an is picking the fig back up. It says, *"By the Fig, by the Olive, and by Mt. Sinai."* Mt. Sinai is the mountain where Moses went up on and G_d spoke to him there; and G_d gave him revelation on Mt. Sinai. Mt. Sinai is referring to ascending up, going higher up to G_d, getting communication from G_d, and then coming back down. The third in this reference is Mt. Sinai, and the fourth reference is the town. The Qur'an says, *"And this town made safe."* How do you make the town safe? You make the town safe by respecting all the people.

Respect for the Common Mind

All of us have imagination but all of us do not have olives. All of us can think and we have vivid imaginations, most of us. So, respect the common mind. I think the fig is symbolic of the common mind. It is a metaphor representing the common mind. Respect the common mind; then, respect those who are looking for a single thought, or a single interest symbolized in the olive. They are focused on one thing. Those are the educated people. They focus on one thing and they stay focused on that until it becomes illuminated, like the oil. You can strike a match near it and get fire. So, they focus on one thing so long until it illuminates for them and then they get the insight. They get the knowledge and they pass it on. These are all stages.

Social Interaction Shows Us How to Apply Knowledge

Then the Qur'an says, *"And the town made safe."* It includes the town, because we have to develop in the town. You can go up on the mountain and you can get all of that good knowledge and good insight, but if you don't come back down and live with people, you will never know how to use it. How do we learn how to communicate with one another? By living with one another. We live with one another and we learn how to communicate with one another. We live with one another, then we know how to apply our knowledge.

It takes this social interaction to show us how to apply knowledge, where to put it, and how to use it. If we never have a chance to socialize, or have social interaction, we will never truly become educated. To have light and not put it to use is no education at all. I am sure when Moses came down from the mountain, he had a great light. But he had to come down and look at his people's circumstances and then see how he was to use that light that G_d gave him on the mountain to see how to apply it; and he wasn't selfish.

Charge Everybody with Responsibility

This is the same Moses who is in the Bible and Qur'an. He is for both of us. He wasn't a selfish man saying, "I'm going to do this by myself." The first thing he did was to look around and see what resources he had. He said, "You doctors get together! You lawyers get together! You farmers get together! You musicians get together." Moses started organizing people according to their skills and abilities, etc. Then, he gave them what G_d gave him from the mountain, and he charged all of them with responsibility to use it, apply it, and make their lives conform to it. We can't do all of that. That is too much for us. We are not Moses. But what we can do is respect everybody, have respect for everybody.

Good Character Required for Healthy Citizenship

Islam begins with the promotion of good character and good character is respect for everything that deserves respect. A person of good character respects your property. You say to a person, "Here is my key. You can use my car to go to the store and pick up some groceries, because you don't have a car." A person of good character will not abuse that trust. He will treat that car just like it was his and even better. If he's such a person who doesn't care too much about a Rolls Royce, it could have been a wagon, but you trusted him with a Rolls Royce.

Therefore, he's going to give the respect that a Rolls Royce deserves, not the respect that a wagon deserves. So, you have to be of good character to have healthy citizenship. The reason why we don't have many people having this kind of serious thought about the great interest that we are entrusted with when we are trusted with the responsibility of citizenship is because we don't have the perception of the country, the city, or town, that most religions give us.

Everything Temporary Except G_d

First of all, everything that we have was not ours to begin with. We came into the world owning nothing. Human beings did not make the land. They found land that could support their life. So, the gift is from G_d, originally, and that is what we have to remember, firstly. And under G_d you are responsible for how you treat everything. You may dislike the government, at times, and may want to say, "Oh, I don't have any citizenship. My citizenship is not worth a plug nickel." You may feel like that, but remember, everything is temporary except G_d. Bad circumstances are temporary, and G_d is not going to excuse you from your responsibility. You are going to have to answer to G_d, one day, and He is not going to excuse you from any responsibility that you should have. Don't look at the land just as government land and as private property. Look at it as land that G_d gave to man, the human being. G_d gave man this land, so, don't look at it as just your possession. G_d gave it to all of us. Therefore, this land we call the United States of America, it was given to all of us, originally. It was the right of all of us. Nobody had established their rights to exclude anybody else. In the beginning, it was the right of all of us.

In so-called primitive tribes and societies, they respect that. They live with each other, but they don't put any claim on land, or rivers, etc. If you use a boat, you can't even claim the boat. Some primitive tribes won't let you claim the boat. The boat is only for traveling the river, and since the river does not belong to anyone, then the boat can't belong to anybody in particular. The boat has to be for anyone who wants to use the boat. If no one is riding on the boat and it is there beside the water, anybody can jump into that boat and use it.

"One Nation Under G_d"

These are people who are still in touch with the first perception of these goods. The first perception is that, "We didn't do this. We didn't provide these things. It was here when we got here, so, we should respect the Original Owner". You should say, "This is my city," and mean it; "New York is my city", and you should mean that from your heart. As I have said, don't let your thinking separate itself from your heart. You should think about it and have that, also, in your heart. "This is my city. G_d did not give this land to one person. It is for human beings and my government has made a beautiful city here. My fellow Americans, have made a beautiful city here and this is my city." Claim it!

Also, under the Constitution of these United States, it says, "One Nation under G_d", and it speaks of a Creator. It says, "We hold these truths to be self-evident that all men are created equal." It is back to the common person and they are, "Endowed with certain inalienable rights...", that you can't take away. They are endowed by their Creator, which means they are created by their Creator with certain inalienable rights; rights that you can't take away from them. "Among these are life, liberty and the pursuit of happiness." It is saying that not even the government can take these rights from a person. The right to life was not given by the government and it cannot be taken away from the person by the government.

G_d Created All Men Equal and Free to Reach Potential

Regarding life and liberty, G_d created us to be free. The government didn't give us that and the government shouldn't take it away. G_d gave us the intelligence, the feet, the hands, and the legs, to go get things we need to pursue happiness and to acquire wealth. The government shouldn't take that away from us. Our government is saying that we have rights that the government didn't give to us and the rights began with the right to life, liberty, and the pursuit of happiness.

So, don't say anymore that, "This school that I attend is their school." I don't care if it is a private school, or if it is the biggest school in the state of California, don't ever go to school and say, "This is their school", no matter how bad you feel, or how bad someone is treating you there. Don't let them take you out of your rights. You need to be situated to be successful and if your psyche is not positive, you will not be able to perform as well. To have a positive psyche you have to be positive and you have to be positive when it is right to be positive; and you have a right to say: "Charlotte is my town. This school I am going to is my school." What do I mean? The wall is mine. The carpet is mine. The lights are mine. Then treat it like it is yours. Respect it. Pick up the paper, when you see trash on the floor. Don't wait for the janitor. If you don't see the janitor, pick it up. I do that out there in the streets, in the public streets. You might say, "There goes a nut!" But I am a healthy nut and I'm a healthy citizen. This is the way to have healthy citizenship. You have to think the way G_d wants us to think. And you have to know that great governments have respected the way G_d wants us to think.

Raising Children in Horrible Environments

We're raising children in an environment where their little young minds are receiving impressions from horrible things that are going on. Some of us have pay per view cable TV and we will leave the television on, go out, and leave our little children in the house and we don't know what they are watching on the television. Consequently, you don't know what is going into their minds, what is shaping their thinking, what is shaping their minds. Then we have, all the time, reports of horrible things. All of this is hurting the young mind. As a result, we have abusers, sometimes, right in the house, abusing the children, killing their sensitivity, making them not care whether they hurt, kill, or not.

So, we should, first, reflect on our own society that is not safe for our children and we should try to do something about that. We should work with those who are working to get pornography off of the cable television, off of pay per view. We should work with those who are trying to make our environment healthier for our young people and for our decent families to save our decent families and keep young people from being exposed to these horrible things.

No Healthy Attention

But, also, we should be with those who are saying, "Violence breeds violence". The news of violence will trigger violence in a poor person who is miserable and wants to hurt somebody. They say misery loves company. They are people who are so miserable they want to make somebody else miserable, not just find a miserable person to have company and be friends with. They want to hurt somebody to have relief. They don't know anything else to do. Their situation won't permit them to say, "Oh, I have to fight this. I have to resist this. This is bad. Though I'm suffering and everything, I should not take it out on anybody else." It is very difficult when you are suffering and nobody is giving you attention.

In many places, where these children live they get no healthy attention. They get no sympathy. They are treated just like they are nothing but beasts or something and that makes them worse, not better. So, first, we should know that children would not behave this way, if the world had not gone to the extremes to which it has gone and become so violent, itself. The world is violent. The news is filled with violence. The movies are filled with violence. There is violence everywhere, and it is breeding violence. So, let us not say, "These horrible boys!" No, let us say, "This horrible environment!"

We Have to Keep Everything Connected

I think the events of September 11, 2001 were a terrible blow to us as citizens. It hurt us in many ways, but it, also, concerted us to help us be better than we were before. When you run into trouble, if you learn from the trouble, you can be better at what you're doing than you were before. So, let us learn from what happened and try to be better than we were before. I would say that we should just support our community, support our schools, and know that without these things we would be much worse off. We are a strong people, because we have strong institutions, government, schools, all of our fine institutions. We should become more aware of them as progress for us. They represent the progress of society, the progress of civilization.

We should think back in time, in history, sometimes. Just reflect. You can do it within a second. Just think, "Man, did not always have schools. We did not always have fire departments. We did not always have police departments. We did not have these things, but we needed these things, and good people have supported these things. That is why we have them, and that is why we have progressed". You see, if we don't remember, we just see these things separate in time; separate, or out of the growth line of the people and their environment. We see them out of that. When you see them out of that, they lose their importance. So, we have to keep everything connected and we have to appreciate what we have as progress. Then we can work better. We can think better. We will have more energy to work with. If you don't keep things together, you just lose the connections, your energy is dissipated, and you can't go forward with your life.

The Devil Is Not Fantasy

Some of us we hear of the devil, Satan, and I think we don't know that it is not fantasy. It is not make-belief. The devil is here, too. The devil is on earth. The devil is among us. The devil is still influencing the world and our life, against us, just as he did the first parents of ours. He came and he influenced their thinking, so he would hurt the way they see truth, so they would get in trouble. And that is still going on. The bigger the world gets the bigger the job for the devil gets, and the bigger his work is.

No Respect for the Head

I remember the dance called, "Breakdancing". The first time I saw it I was angered by that dance, because I did not just see a dance, children doing something. I saw the works of the devil. Here was a dance called, breakdancing. Do you think children called it breaking? Do you think they named it breakdancing? They didn't name it that. Some devil suggested to them the name, "Breaking, or "breakdancing". The youth, they would spin on their heads. The expression, "He had that little guy spinning on his head," means that he had him completely out of control and he was completely in control of a person who had him spinning on his head. It means, "I've got him completely out of control and I'm the one controlling him". That's Satan!

What are you doing when you're spinning on your head? You are showing no respect for your head. The head is the highest point on your body. It represents your height, your progress. And the progress is represented in your thinking, what you have learned, etc. Now, you are using it for a spinning top, spinning on your head calling it, "Breaking". I'm not making humor. I'm not making jokes. I'm very serious. This thing was inspired by the devil, the Satan, himself; breaking, or breakdancing. Satan is telling us, "I'm going to have your whole society spinning on its head and breaking down, not building up".

Fight the Schemes of Satan

How should we look at horrible things that our young people do? Look at it as it was inspired by Satan. He has made the environment speak these things to the minds of our young people and we have to fight Satan. How do we fight Satan? We fight his works. And in our Qur'an, G_d says, *"Fight the schemes of Satan, for his schemes are weak"*.[18] If you use your good heart and your good human intelligence, you will be able to see what he is doing. Now, let us fight what he is doing. Let us defeat Satan. Get him out of our lives. The Bible says rebuke him and he will run! He is not invincible! He can be whipped!

Chapter 2

Coming to the Qibla of the Muslims

Al-Fatiha (the first chapter of the Qur'an) is the key for us understanding how the major issues of Scripture should be dealt with, and how they should be perceived. It is, also, a connection with the Old Testament that shows how Al-Fatiha addresses the Old Testament to introduce the whole of the Qur'an. The whole of the Qur'an is about fulfilling, or establishing the purpose of G_d's Word. The battle is not over. The victory has not been won.

The Bible came. The Torah came. The Injeel (the Gospel) came and the Jews carried out their plan and tried to go to the destiny. The Christians came up and they claimed they had the new destiny. They are trying to get to the destiny. But never did they get to where they are now, to have the beautiful democracy we have in America, without the help of the Qur'an, Muhammed, and Islam.

It is proven that the Qur'an came and connected our minds, the minds of the bright stars in the people; connected their minds with the Bible's progression of the work to deliver man to his G_d in beautifully formed society; to have the kingdom come on earth as it is in heaven. The work to do that is continued by the Qur'an under Muhammed, the Prophet, and the work is to establish man in a beautiful life form; as an individual and as a society in the beautiful life form planned for man by G_d, Himself. I repeat, it had not been realized, though the Torah was being lived, or practiced by Jews, and the Gospel by Christians. But instead of them realizing that bright day in the future of mankind, the whole world had come, again, under darkness. Is that not true? This is history. This is not just Scripture and the Bible says, *"It is a famine of hearing the word of G_d".*[19]

We Hear and We Obey

Hearing means understanding. It doesn't just mean sound reaching your ears. *"Hear ye the Word of G_d and live"*. It doesn't just mean to get the sound in your ears. It means heed what you hear, obey what you hear. G_d says, in the Qur'an, *"Sami'naa wa a-ta'naa, we hear and we obey; to hear is to obey"*.[20] There was no obedience, that is what it means. Nobody was hearing and knowing how to correctly obey the Word of G_d. Nowhere in the world, no nation had it. Isn't that where we are, again, today?

Except for a few countries, the whole Islamic world has fallen under darkness. Saudi Arabia, where the sacred precincts are, the rulers there, they are not doing justice by their citizens. They are not helping to straighten out the problems we have in this world. They are contributing to them, giving us more problems and do not show any repentance. We don't hear the cry of a sincere worshiper of G_d coming out of Saudi Arabia; a lover of humanity. We don't hear that voice coming out of Saudi Arabia. We look all over the Islamic world and we can't hear it. They are all tied up in their small troubles. So, that is a time like that for Islam.

A Trustee Formed by G_d

In terms of human measurements, how big can the human being become? You cannot become a god. Allah made us human, not gods. You cannot become an angel. We're human, not angels. But the human measurement is so big that the leader of the angels (as given to us in the Qur'an) became very jealous, when G_d told the angels that He was creating man (the human being) for leadership. The leader of the angels became so jealous that he rebelled against G_d. G_d says to the angels, according to our holy book, He said, *"Surely, I am making, in the earth, a khalifah"*.[21] Now, we can translate this word, khalifah, in different ways, as a trustee, as a ruler; as one who is given responsibility of rule, or to fix the rule; to fix the order, or to fix the authority. But it is as a trustee, not as the authority, himself; as a trustee formed by G_d to keep the trust.

The Scholars Made a Mistake

We know that in the history of Islam we had khalifahs (khulafaah), who came, after the passing away from this earth of Muhammed, the Prophet, peace be upon him (pbuh), who was the Messenger of G_d. And the first successor after him that the Muslim community looked to as their leader was called, khalifah, Abu Bakr As-Siddeeq. And the four great khalifs, we know as Abu Bakr, Omar, Uthman and Ali. They were the four great rulers after Muhammed, the Prophet. I believe persons who have studied, very seriously, what developed after the leadership of our Prophet, I believe that it wasn't necessarily those individuals that made the mistake. But I think the scholars made a mistake in the identifying of individual persons as khalifah.

Now, I know this is a concern to those in Islamic circles of knowledge, the teachers, imams, scholars, etc. But I have said it to an audience of honorable and highly respected scholars, so, I'm not saying this, secretly. I was saying this to them in their own country what I'm saying right now. I think, if we study the history, we will see that a mistake was made in identifying individuals as khalifah.

The Collective Body Must Be the Rule

G_d says, in our holy book, the Qur'an, He's making on earth a khalifah. I am of the understanding that G_d was saying that every human being is a potential khalifah and we can have that rule that G_d entrusted to the khalifah, together, not separately. It has to be together as a collective body, that we can be khalifah; not in a single person. The collective body must be the rule. Prophet Muhammed, himself, refused to accept to rule, although he was chosen as the Messenger and servant of Allah. G_d had made him an authority in our lives, but he refused to accept to give orders and not have others use their own minds and thinking to contribute to a decision, or a choice in matters. He invited his companions, his learned people who were in his company, to think on their problems, or their situations, and give him their opinions. He would say: "What do you have to say about this, Khalid ibn Waleed?"

Islam Governed by Democratic Process

He would turn to one and then turn to another, asking their opinion, their advice. G_d was communicating the Qur'an to him, directly, but he still respected the opinion of others. He didn't want to make any decision by himself, unless G_d had revealed that decision in Qur'an. He wanted to have others join him in arriving at the conclusion and making the right decision.

This tells me that Islam is governed by consensus, by democratic process. Islam has respect for the intelligence of other people and one person can never make all the decisions, because that merely shows that he has no respect for the intelligence of other people. We accept the hadith (sayings of Muhammed, the Prophet) that says the control of G_d is on the collective body; which means that G_d is not governing the people through one person. But G_d wants a government by and for a collective body; not one individual.

We know that G_d says to us, as Muslims, "You are a community," and community is a collective body. He didn't say you are individuals, or you are a priesthood. He said, *"You are a community evolved, or raised up for the good of all people"*.[22] You are the best, resourceful, community in terms of how you can benefit others. You are the most useful and the most productive of communities evolved by G_d. And the Word of G_d evolved the ummah (community) of Islam and evolved it for the good of all people.

A Place That belongs to All people

The qibla is the direction for us for our prayer. The house called, Ka'bah, it is not an Arab qibla. It is on Arab land, but it is not an Arab qibla. It's not an Arab sacred point, or place. It is a designating direction for us in prayer and Hajj, the Pilgrimage. It is a place that belongs to all people. G_d says that it was built for all humanity, for all mankind. It was built by the Prophet Abraham, or Ibraheem, as it is pronounced in the Qur'anic, or the Arabic language. We know of Abraham. Like the Bible tells us, G_d made Abraham father of all nations and our holy book says He made Abraham, peace be upon the Prophet, a leader for all the nations. The Ka'bah was built for all people and it was built by the one who G_d said He made a leader for all people.[23]

Prophet Muhammed Ended Nationalism

So, you know, we can't have any narrow nationalism, or make our religion nationalistic. We can't do that and Muhammed, the Prophet, in his farewell address, he told the people there is no superiority of an Arab over a non-Arab and no superiority of a non-Arab over an Arab. He ended nationalism. There's no nationalistic comfort in Islam. The purpose is to make human society obey under the direction that G_d intended for every human being, so that every human being will be in an environment, or in circumstances that favor them growing up to the full measurement that G_d wants for the human person. And the full measurement is told in many ways. The people of the book are refusing to acknowledge something that is great. But though it is not acknowledged by them, Muhammed's qibla is the better qibla for all people, in their churches, in their synagogues, in their religions.

Collective Rule and Authority

It has been acknowledged by them in their search for the ideal society; how to establish the best government for the people. I believe France was first to think, "What is the best form of government for us to have for all people to have progress and fewer problems than we have with these other forms of governments we have experienced?" Their thinkers arrived at the idea of collective rule, collective authority, that we now call, democracy.

Our democracy, in these United States, comes to birth upon a perception of the human being as a creation with rights that you can't take away from him. You can't violate these rights and these rights belong to each human person that is accepted in the citizenry, by virtue of their own natural composition. They have these rights, simply, because they are human. The identity is human. So, if the identity is human, they are entitled to these rights by virtue of their own identity and composition, not made by man, not made by government; but it is inherent, in the very flesh of every person.

Coming to the Qibla of the Muslims

This is the position the great philosophers took and we have this idea holding our political concept together; the belief in the inalienable rights of the individual human person. Once you accept to be a citizen here (America), you have that recognition and those rights cannot to be taken from you by anybody. Consequently, no government, nobody, can take those rights from any individual human person.

So, our government, France, and other Western governments that have that as an adhesive holding that ideology together, those governments have come to the qibla (orientation, direction for alignment) of the Muslims. That is exactly what we believe. Those who put together that idea for us for generations to come, I'm sure they understood that this applied, also, to the collective body of the people; that it is more important as a possession of the human community than it is as a possession of the human individual.

Spirit for the Human Community

What we inherit is the community spirit, the spirit for the human community. We are not just inheriting properties that are to be established as the properties of individual human life. No! We are inheriting an urge, a spirit, a direction in our life that will connect us with others who have the same; and the purpose of it is for us to form a social community, a community of people. That is why G_d says in the Qur'an, highly glorified is He, that there are creatures that go about on this earth and they have communities like yours. That is to tell us that it is not only a description of humans. This is the description of life, period![24]

You don't have to stretch your imagination too much to agree with those who say even plant life exists in communities. Grass wants to be with grass, trees with trees. That is the forest, isn't it? If you don't have the right qibla and your life has been interrupted and confused by the world that rejects the real qibla, or is ignorant of the real qibla, you will be unconscious in your own nature. It will be unconscious in your own makeup to come to that idea, or that belief, that recognition, that, "I am human and I should mate with other humans".

To Be Human Is Your Sacred Property

If a black person is not human and you are black, the human shouldn't mate with the non-human. Human is first, not Africa, not Europe; not white, or black; yellow, or red. That is your valuable property that you are human. That is your sacred property that you are human. It would be better that you are human and keep your own identity with your people. But if all of your people turn to another qibla that makes them wild and crazy, filthy and inhuman, then you should leave all of your people and become white, yellow, red, or anything else, rather than give up your humanity. This is where we should be when we're reading the Qur'an and reading about Muhammed's excellent model. His excellent model is not an Arab. His excellent model is the pure human type G_d wants in every human being walking on the earth.

If G_d had awakened him up in his Arab identity and fastened him to his Arab identity, he never would have been known. He would have gotten nowhere. But G_d didn't wake up Muhammed, the Prophet (peace be upon him), in his Arab identity. G_d woke him up in his human identity and G_d gives us a sign, a qibla (house) that identifies us with our original nature, our original life, our original human pattern that G_d planned for all people.

Muhammed Established the First Democratic Republic

What Muhammed, the Prophet, was blessed by G_d to establish was the first democratic republic to re-people, renew, again. Democratic means fair, where everybody will be able to participate; no one person dictating, or bossing everybody. The people participate. It is a mutual consensus. It is a mutual decision that they all agree in, or accept. This is Qur'an.

It is by consultation, mutually consulting one another to come up with the best that each other can offer and then presenting what the people came up with, what they concluded was the better for them and establishing that as the decision, the resolution, or the order. If you are a Muslim and you're educated, went to college and graduated, and you can't understand that being a democratic republic, you are telling me that you don't like your own religion; because to deny the beauty of your own religion shows me you don't like your own religion.

America's Founders Borrowed from Muhammed

The Founding Fathers, they consulted the best of knowledge and the best of books. They consulted the best of leaders that the earth had produced. The cleanest and the most successful of the leaders, they consulted them. The most productive of nations, the most productive of political orders, they searched to find them, to see, "What can we expect? What can we take from the past that proved itself and use it to make ours the best?" That is what they did. So, don't think they didn't borrow from Muhammed, the Prophet. They borrowed a lot from him. I'm talking about the founders of this great nation. They borrowed a lot from the Qur'an even public education and love for education.[25]

Public Education Began with Muhammed's Teachings

Actually, public education began with Muhammed, the Prophet's teachings. There was no public education before and this modern world didn't have public education, until very recently in its history. Isn't that a fact? Public education is a recent development, even for the West. Prophet Muhammed started public education. From the time that he received the revelation of the Qur'an he made education a duty on every citizen, male and female, as G_d guided him. He obligated every person who learned a little of the Qur'an, the wisdom, the sciences, etc., to teach it to another; to take it to another person no matter how little they had. "The world is in darkness. Your neighbors all around you are in ignorance. So, if you have a little bit, take it to them. They are in need of it! Everybody is in need of it! Take it to them. Don't have them in darkness anymore. Don't wait until you get a Ph.D. You already have one line of the master wisdom. You've got one line, one verse, one ayah (verse) of the master wisdom, the supreme wisdom; the highest knowledge, the highest science. So, don't wait until you get a Ph.D. Take that to that man whose brain is starving, dead, dusty. Take that to him, so he will have some sense and be educated. Let the education process begin with the first line of revelation." That was the Prophet. Spread it to every member of the society, so that the whole public has it. That was Muhammed, the Prophet. You can understand that being a revolution; a revolution, a cultural revolution, a spiritual revolution. But, eventually, it was a total revolution.

"Oh People! Lend Me Your Ears!"

We get the word from Muhammed, the Prophet, in the tenth year after the Hijra (migration from Mecca to Madinah),[26] in about the twenty-second, or twenty-third year of his life as the last Prophet, the seal of the Prophets. This was near the end of his life with us on this earth. And he said, "Oh, people!" Now, couldn't he have said, "Oh, Muslims?" How would we have said it? I don't think we would say, "Oh, people", if we had gotten a big victory like that after thirteen years of suffering persecution, being put down and being kept out of the Sacred Mosque; denied the permission to make pilgrimage; and all of a sudden, G_d had blessed us to be victorious, with an army too big for the enemy to deal with. I don't think most of us would have done what the Prophet did (even the best, or most saintly of us). I don't think we could have looked out at that great multitude of our followers, of our members and said, "Oh, people!" We would have said, "Oh, Muslims! Oh, Muslim victors that have vanquished the kafirs (disbelievers)!" That's how we would have done it and we would have preached and preached and preached in that spirit. But the Prophet, he knew they were Muslims. He knew they were believers. He knew that they had been converted by G_d, or converted by his efforts under G_d, to the religion of Islam. But he didn't say, "Oh, Muslims!" or, "Oh, believers!" No, he didn't. He said, "Oh, people!" "Oh, people", he said, "Listen to me!" Isn't that wonderful? "Oh, people! Listen to me!"

Here is a man that has such excellent, perfect, human character. He is the victor. The average one of us would not get there and say, "Listen to me." We would just begin to talk and if they didn't listen, we would say, "Go over there and chop his head off! Hey, that one over there is not listening to me, so, go over there and chop his head off! Shoot that son of a gun!" Yes, if we had that kind of victory and power, we would be crazy with our power. But he said, "Oh, people" and then asked them, like the Roman, "Lend me your ears."; "Lend me your ears", like the Roman emperor, who said, "Friends, Romans, countrymen, lend me your ears".[27]

The Prophet was supposed to have been uneducated, a child that never got formal education. He was raised to that high station by G_d and didn't have the background of the Romans, in their knowledge and their cultural excellence; although they were savages on one side. They were like that guy in a movie that I saw. On one side, you saw a presentable human being and on the other side you saw a beast. I don't know what happened over there in Europe, but something happened. It looks like they couldn't get the whole body into civilization. One side would be civilized and the other side would be savage; a monster on the one half and a human being on the other half. We understand that condition. Believe me, G_d has blessed us to understand that condition and He healed us. We don't have to suffer that. He said, "All praise is for Allah." He didn't claim praise. He let them know, right away, that the credit for the victory goes to G_d. He said:

> "All praise is for Allah. We praise Him, seek Him, seek His pardon, and we turn to Him. We seek refuge with Allah for the evils of our soul and from the evil consequences of our deeds. Whom Allah guides aright, there is none to lead him astray and there is none to guide him whom Allah leads astray."

You may say, "Would G_d lead a person astray?" Yes, if G_d gives you mercy and guidance and has patience with you, has mercy on you and pardons you over and over again, the very thing that was meant to guide you aright will then be changed and it will be your guide to hell. But you will have brought that on yourself, not G_d. Then he said:

> "And there is none to guide aright whom Allah leads astray. I bear witness that there is no god but Allah, the only One. He fulfilled His promise to and granted victory to His servants and He, Alone, routed the enemies."[28]

He didn't say, "I'm your general. I am the victor, here." He didn't say to his army, "Under your general, we have defeated them. We have routed them." He said, "G_d routed the enemy. G_d defeated the enemy. G_d hemmed them in. G_d brought them down. G_d vanquished them". G_d did it.

The Proper Treatment of Women

The Prophet delivered this last sermon, or this last speech to the multitudes on Mount 'Arafat; and those who have made Hajj, like I have, you have visited Mount 'Arafat, I'm sure. That is where our Prophet spoke and I'm sure the guides there guided you to just where he stood, on a raised level there where he stood and delivered his speech. There, on 'Arafat, the Prophet went on to address the treatment of women and, also, the treatment of slaves. And what he said, in effect, was that women have been held back from their dignity, their G_d-given respect, dignity, inherent value and honor, and men have been responsible for it. Men have imposed themselves upon women and denied them their rights as equal human beings with men. Did you hear what I said? "Equal human beings with males", that's what the Prophet said, in effect. The Prophet appealed, very earnestly, to the men to accept the responsibility to correct that wrong and to treat their women with the proper respect and to recognize their women's rights to engage in business, to inherit wealth from their parents; to be educated, to participate in the vital processes and have roles in the vital institutions of the society; to have a public voice that would enable them to influence the state and the course of the state, or the nation. This is what our Prophet did along with what G_d revealed.

Muhammed Made It Impossible for Slavery to Continue

Muhammed, the Prophet, the seal of the Prophets, he made it impossible for slavery to continue. He didn't prohibit people from having servants. You could have servants, but not that servant that is the typical slave whose ego has been crushed, whose sense of personal value has been destroyed; and who thinks that you, now, are an almighty in his life. He did away with that. "You can't have servants as your property anymore. The servant is not your property. He's G_d's creation. He belongs to G_d. You want to keep him as your servant? All right, feed him the food you, yourself, eat."

This is what the Prophet said and that goes a long way. "Feed your servants the food you, yourself, eat and dress him in the clothes you, yourself, wear! And don't say to him, 'My slave'. But say to him, 'My dependent'". It means that he is like a child, depending on you for certain needs. But he's not your slave. In other words, treat him like you would your own child from your wife and from your own loins. That's what the Prophet was saying. Treat him like you would your own child from your own loins and from your wife. Treat him like that. Don't say, "My slave". He said, "Don't say, 'Abdi (slave)'." This is the Prophet's teaching.

Feed Him the Food You Eat

It is reported that one man said, asking about what the Prophet said, "What did he say regarding the slave?" They told him that he said you have to feed him the food you, yourself, eat and you have to clothe him in the clothes you, yourself, wear. And you have to make education a possibility for him just like you make it a possibility for your own children. He said, "What! Why, I don't want my slave, anymore!" And that was the purpose. That was just what it was designed to do. It was designed to make the slaveowner, or the slave master become fed up and not find it desirable, anymore, to own slaves.

"Oh, it is not desirable, anymore, to have him as my slave. I have to feed him the food that I eat? Now, I'm going to buy lamb chops, today, and he's got to eat some lamb chops? I wear these clothes, here that cost a little money and I can't give the clothes that I throw away, anymore, the tattered rags that I throw away? I can't let him find sandals on the roadside that someone threw away? Well, I don't want him anymore! He's not profitable. It is no more businesslike, or profitable to keep him!"

As a result, many of them gave up slaves right away. And those who kept slaves their slaves were not slaves, anymore, by our definition of what a slave is. They were working, or were employed in the employment of that person to do certain jobs. But they were respected and embraced as brothers and sisters. They would greet them, "As-Salaam Alaikum, brother." They treated them as members of their own household, as family members.

The Prophet went on and made it an obligation that a slave, or a black man, had to be respected as having the right to qualify for ascension in government and no office was barred against him. No office was restricted. The slave could rise up as high as he wanted to go. The Prophet said, "If a slave of Africa becomes your leader, you must respect and follow him". That means that a slave of Africa, a black man, or a slave, has the right to become the leader of all the Muslims. He referred to a slave of Africa, with black skin and nappy hair, and he made it plain that he wasn't talking about one with straight hair; i.e., an Arab, or an Asian, living in Africa. He made it plain he was talking about a person who had been a slave and, also, was black with nappy hair. He made that very clear. He said, "If that person becomes your leader, if he follows the Qur'an and the Prophet's way, then obey him." This is what the Prophet said.

The Western Idea of the Destiny Is Islamic

Now, we have the language, "Destiny". We know it, because the Christian world used it and popularized it. Too often, Muslims frown on anything the West says. "Oh, the Imam sounds like the Western thinkers when he is talking about destiny." And, some of the big ulema, the big chiefs, the big thinkers in Islam, I know they have said this of me. They say, "He's coming from the Western idea, when he says, "Destiny". No, I'm not! I'm coming from the Islamic idea and if anything, the West copied Islam, when it gave its idea of the destiny; that man should work for the destiny, should hope for the destiny and should order his society so it is realized for him as the destiny. Is this a Western idea? Certainly, it is. This is a Western democracy. Those that were working over here for the destiny, in the literature, they called it, the manifest destiny, meaning something that had not been seen, yet; something that they wanted to realize, that they wanted to see; that they wanted to have materialize in their eyes and for their life. Now, you know, for real Christians, America has not come to any manifest destiny, yet. This is not the destiny yet. They still hope to see the destiny. But progress has been made towards the destiny and any of us that can't see that we are dumb and in the dark ourselves. They have made great progress towards the destiny in spite of the sins and corruption and the duplicity in the character, morals and the make-up of this society; that show us a devil on one side and an angel on the other side; righteousness on one side and wickedness on the other side; a system to support the righteous and a system to support the criminals. We know all of that exists. But, we know that is not what the real Christian wants. And we know that is not what the true, decent, American citizens want. That's why they fight crime. That is why they fight lies. That is why they fight corruption, and why they fight immorality. They fight all of these things as decent American citizens, because that is not what they want.

Chapter 3

Sharing America's Freedom Space

Muhammed, the Prophet of Islam, was like Moses, and Jesus is as a sign pointing to Muhammed, the Prophet. Muhammed's ummah, or his community, is the community of Abraham. Abraham was a man of rational faith. So, his community is not a spiritual community. Muhammed's community is not a spiritual community. That's not the description for it. Yes, we are a spiritual people. We have our spirituality. We have spiritual interests, etc., or spiritual life. But we, by description, are not a spiritual community. We are a social community. And that's what is told in the sheep in Scripture.

Abraham's son is shown as a sheep. And a sheep means, or has reference to a community that is strong in its social nature, constituted socially in a very strong, strong way. That's all the sheep is symbolic of. That's the meaning for the sheep. Now, the predicament for the sheep in the world you can't understand it, until G_d makes the sheep, man. The sheep has to become man; that is, G_d has to give him position, authority, and rule in the world. The sheep's life is threatened and his situation in the world is very, very insecure.

People of Scripture Destined to Have Own Social Order

World leaders fear nothing more than a development in obedient people to G_d that is social. They don't want you to have your social life, not in their social order. We have a democracy, now, that I think can accommodate other social orders in its social order. I do believe that. But the world, the governments of yesterday, they would not tolerate any other social orders. You could have your spiritual order, but not your social order; not in their government.

That's why there was so much fighting between the religious people and the worldly people; so many wars, religious wars they say. The world wouldn't tolerate you having your own community, or your own social order. And that's what it's saying, that the destiny for the people of Scripture is that they should have their own community life; their own social order. They are not to live in the social sciences, or in the social order of the world. They're to establish their life upon the social order that G_d reveals.

People Avoiding Responsibility in Social Order Cannot be Free

People avoiding their responsibility in the social order cannot be free. You may act as though you're free. You may think as though you are free. But you cannot be truly free, not in a world made by man, or any other world in fact, if you are avoiding your own social responsibility. Freedom is a reward for hard work. In the wilds, where animals are free, freedom is not protected. The survival of the fittest is the law, although individual man is thousands of years away from the animal law. But that condition can form in the freedom space of those who go about carefree and the animal law will be their dead-end street. For freedom, the wilds had to be defeated. The first to be defeated were wild animals and unprincipled people. Heavy responsibility was carried by parents. This is how the world began rising as civilized society.

Public Has to Have Citizenship Knowledge

Neighbors were not able to go it alone, so, the neighbors had to band together working for the common interest. Laws were put in place. Public land was developed and schools were opened to have life assisted by practical knowledge. To make it, to live through the raw, savage times, neighbors worked as a family of partners in the rise of civilization. Today, in modern times, to know the reality of populations surviving to have more citizenship knowledge is indispensable. They have to have citizenship knowledge. Life not understood cannot be vouchsafed and cannot get protection under the law.

Home Grown Benefits

Intelligent laws reach the public as home grown benefits like almost every other public good. We forget the home. We forget how everything we have can open society. A good of any real, true, value, it really is home grown. It was developed at home before it was introduced to the public. Our cooking, our diets, the way we prepare our food, the things that are good for us in the market, today; the way to cook, prepare the food; and, we can include, also, clothing, the making of clothing; it all started at home. We can include, also, health remedies. Medicine had its beginning in the home and if you can stretch your mind a little bit, government, also, had its beginning in the home, because family developed, naturally. Family had a sense of order. It had a sense of authority. Its authority was in the parents. The father was seen as the number one authority. But in the home, or at home, the mother was seen as being the person in charge of that freedom space. Family is the form of government that we need.

Even Animals Respect Rights of Other Animals

Animals respect the rights of other animals. If you have had any animals, or pets, I am sure that you know that. But if you have not had any, if you have just observed animals, birds find food and then, other birds follow them. The other birds are, perhaps, bigger, or stronger. They could easily drive the other birds away; but we find among them a respect. A few birds are so greedy and desperate they just take over. But most birds will come and if the birds that arrived, first, refuse to permit them to eat, they will wait until the first group of birds eat a little bit and they start to be less defensive;

then that later group will come in and eat; not only birds, cats, dogs, and chickens. I have observed in animals that they respect the rights of each other.

Children Insist That Their Rights be Respected

Children insist that their rights be respected. You do not have to teach children this. They come up with a sense that is ingrained, and it is inborn sense. They come up with a sense of their own rights. So, if you take something from them that they have and they know it was not for you, it is theirs, they do not like that. They will protest. They will cry. If they can, they will even fight you. So, there is an inborn sense. There is an inherent sense of one's rights and this was recognized by the framers of the Constitution of these United States. The rights of every citizen are protected by these words. "We hold these truths to be self-evident that all men are created equal (or that all men are born equal) and are endowed with certain unalienable rights." That means rights that cannot be taken from them. "Among these are life, liberty, and the pursuit of happiness."

The Pursuit of Happiness

In a college course, if you take any courses in social science, political science, the class material, or the professor will bring it to the students' awareness that the pursuit of happiness is to be interpreted as the right to own your own property; the right to have a piece of land; the right to have your home on that land; and the right to property if you can afford it. And we know that when the West was being opened up, or developed in the early days of the development of the United States, or this country, its towns and cities, they had so much land that they would grant land to individuals and, also, to poor individuals. They called them, homesteads.

A homestead was a piece of land on which they could have a house, or buildings. Sometimes, the homestead was so big you could have more than a house. And it was expected that they would farm some of that land, because the government wanted food produced and that would be the requirement that they use the land, also, for farming.

At this point, I would like to bring something to our attention, because we have just been pampered, made to expect that we do not have to do anything; that somebody in the government is going to take care of us and do everything for us. We are here just to enjoy life, have fun; eat, sleep; have sex, and die; just like common animals. But we are worse off, because most animals have a sense of social responsibility; responsibility to the children, loyalty to their mate that they mate with to have children; and a sense of responsibility for the land; or the freedom space that they use. Whether it is a bird building a nest in a tree, or animals living in the wild, they have by nature this sense of respect and responsibility.

Public Space Owned by the Citizens of the Public

Children are sharing, sometimes, their freedom space at the table and one will be taking too much off the table. These can be very little children and the other one will say, "You'd better leave me some," because they know it is supposed to be shared. It is not for one of them just to take it over. No, it is shared. They can be in the bedroom. One will have a bunk bed on one side of the room and the other has a bunk bed on the other side of the room and one is disrespecting the freedom space of the other. He's throwing his stuff on the bed of the other one and he will say, "Get this stuff off of my bed!" He is speaking from his soul. He is speaking from rights that are inherent, inborn. Who owns the public space in the United States of America? We do, the members of the United States public, America's public. Who owns the White House that the president lives in? We do. We should understand, or at least come to know our ownership rights. When we work and pay taxes we contribute to all these things.

The local town, its strength, survival, and progress, the state we live in; everything is supported by the more productive people. It is supported by their taxes. And those who are not productive, who don't care to do anything, the money of the productive ones goes to help them; with charity, government assistance; whatever you want to call it. These are realities that a conscious few of us must know in order to help others. Everybody does not have to know what I am giving you here. We only need a conscious few.

An Inherent Need in the Human Being's Soul

Then you become your brother's keeper. You become your sister's keeper. You become the ones who are the guardians in the society. Society needs volunteers. Society needs guardians. People cannot be left alone. We all are not fortunate in the same degree to respect our human intelligence, to respect the inherent sense of the need to produce. That is an inherent need in the human being. It is in the soul. It registers on the mind, if circumstances favor the mind developing.

Sometimes, you can be put in circumstances that will destroy your human intelligence, retard your human senses. The same conditions that affect one individual in that way will affect another one in just the opposite way. They will defy the circumstances. They will defy the conditions that are hurting their intelligence in denying their good life from coming forth and they are the ones who will be our leaders. G_d has made life so that there is always a part of that life, or some in that life who will not accept to go down. No matter how powerful the circumstances are for taking that life, they will not go down, but rise up against it; and they are the leaders.

So, we need something in us, in our minds and our hearts. That is where the true patriot is. He, or she, is a person who lives with something very special as an understanding, as a meaning of what it is to be a citizen of America. And they live with that in their minds and in their hearts. Their spirit is formed of that and they make sure they have children who succeed them. I mean common families. I am not talking about the rich. This is the rich and the poor, the haves and have nots. Among the poor, there are some real patriots very devoted to the best that this country offers and the best traditions that this country offers and they will not separate from it.

They will make sure that their children understand and appreciate it. They lose, sometimes, a child or two and, sometimes, even more. Sometimes, they will lose all of their children; not a one is alive. In their hearts and minds it worries them, but they die with dignity, with strength and they are just happy that they shared it with someone who wasn't their child; with another friend; or with those who would open their ears and invite what they were offering.

The Need to Claim Our Rights

When I began as the leader for the Nation of Islam,[29] I said to myself, "There is no way for us to achieve what we want to achieve in this country if we do not to do what the rest of the blacks, especially, what the civil rights leaders were asking our people to do; and that is claim our rights". Do not have people tell you, "You are not included! You can try but you will not make it! You can invest, but you'll never see what you're after!"

The law should govern the people. What they say in the authority should be respected by them. When I was just starting out as the leader, I said, "If they do not respect it, it does not weaken it. It takes nothing from the law, if they do not respect it. The whole white race might not have respect for it. If I know how to read it, the law is above the people, all of the people, until they get the majority of the people to change it. And as long as they cannot change it with the majority of people that all stands; the authority stands."

I said to myself, "I do not care what they think of me. They may think that I am not worthy of being included as a citizen, or being worthy of the rights and privileges of citizenship. I do not care, as long as I know there is a law that says I should have it. Until they change that, I am going to live as though this country belongs to me as much as it belongs to any other person." I made my decision, long ago, and I said, "This is the psychological disposition that all of us need, if we are to succeed in getting our share of this country." That was my determination. And don't think that G_d was not with me. There was not a time when I did not ask G_d to be with me. I cannot remember any time. My mother could put a whipping on you, when you made her angry, or disappointed her. And when I thought she was coming at me, I called on G_d. So, I said to myself, "I have to work" and I began. I even worked with the children in the school and I set a time when I could speak to them on what they had rights to. I was over the school, at that time, on Stony Island Avenue, in Chicago that was called, the University of Islam (later changed to Clara Muhammad School).

Human Rights Are From G_d

This goes back before the time of the United States, this kind of perception of your entitlement; what you are entitled to as a creature of G_d on this that man did not make. The Creator made it. It goes back to that time before governments. In Islam and in the Qur'an, that is where the language of the scholars came from. They formed their language upon the studies of the Qur'an, what G_d has revealed. Every man, created, is entitled to what G_d created.

There is no means to discriminate against him based upon anything but justice. You can't deny him.

It used to hurt me and it still kind of hurts me to know how the poor Indians, with bows and arrows and little hatchets, how they were just overpowered by European settlers; and how they, eventually, lost their land. It was taken from them and they were put on reservations and told, "Stay on that reservation. If you come off of there, you will have no rights and no protection." They dictated their life to them and confined them to certain restricted areas of land. That hurt me. But what I have learned about our reality is that as products of the earth, we say G_d created us, but we, ourselves, are products of the earth. And obviously, we are special products of the earth that have the ability to use the earth and even alter the picture of the earth that we get.

Muhammed Passed the Test Before Revelation Came

But we can't do that without G_d. We cannot find the vision, the blueprint for establishing our life under G_d, our society under G_d that G_d wants for all people, without G_d revealing to us. So, G_d took the one who was still the excellent Muslim in his nature and had lived that excellent life for forty years, Muhammed Ibn Abdullah. That means he kept his human excellence through the years of puberty when the sex drives are the strongest. He kept it through his manhood when his interest in the world was the strongest, when he had to get food for himself and food for his wife, etc. He kept it through that time. So, he passed the test. Moses fasted forty days. Muhammed fasted for forty years, a lifetime and G_d gave him the revelation for the world. That's Muhammed, the Prophet.[30]

What is the Prophet? The Qur'an says, *"He is a mortal human being, like us".*[31] That means he did not know everything. Some things were out of his reach. He could not know what was in the hearts of people, all the time. Once, someone accused someone and they brought it to Prophet Muhammed and they wanted him to make a decision. They were accusing this person and they were saying that he had taken something. But Prophet Muhammed had no evidence to go upon. So, he told them, "G_d has not given me the power to see inside someone's stomach". Now, the person wasn't talking about food, but the Prophet meant, "He says he has this. I can't see inside of him and see what is in him. If he ate some grapes, I can't look inside and say, 'Yeah, I see some of this and still some is not quite digested, yet'." No, he was not given supernatural powers.

Islamic Democracy Is Consultation

He was a mortal just like us and many times, when he was fighting to establish Islam against the persecutors of the religion, armies were persecuting the religion and Muhammed, the Prophet, he didn't know. He didn't feel comfortable making a battle decision without consulting other men in the army. So, he would consult others in the army and he asked them, "What should we do in this case?" And it proved that there is a possibility that, sometimes, the best advisors who have experience in the world, the fighters, the army, the soldiers, cannot be better than the Prophet that G_d is guiding; because they suggested something and it turned out it didn't work out well.

But the Prophet accepted that it wasn't their fault that it was done. The Prophet accepted it to establish what? He accepted it to establish that we are mortals. We don't know everything. Only G_d knows everything and we need the help of other mortals like us. And though, sometimes, the one person may have the better decision for the most cases, you need to consult others. And since you do for the most cases, consult them in every case.

So, Allah says, *"And orders, or decision-making for the believers, is by consultation amongst you, between each other. You consult each other".*[32] The best minds and the best characters for this particular interest or purpose, consult them. And when you come to a consensus, what the majority of us say, then you follow that. So, we are a democratic society and we will follow that. We won't deviate from that. I'm speaking in the name of this community of Muslims in America. We will follow that. We won't deviate from that. We won't be satisfied until we have that Islamic democracy that Allah wants for us and that respect for the worth and resources of all the good people in our community; where we include them in charting the way for us and building this great society that we're destined to build.

Death of the Whole Society

Unfortunately, the picture of world leaders, today, is shameful. Whether the picture we are looking at is the picture of the Asian world, European world, African world, or the American people, we are looking at a very shameful picture. I recall, in my childhood, older women while they were observing the behavior of a child. They would say, "That boy is rotten to the core". Now, we should never become rotten to the core. We have in our Holy Book, the Qur'an, the saying, *"Your death and your resurrection is like unto that of a single soul."*[33] The more our world works to mute human innocence, the more it gives itself to the moral corruption of the human thought processes. Soon, the loss of purity will bring on the death of the whole society.

The Whole World Under a Curse

We know there are the living still walking the earth, but when we look at the general picture, or the big picture, the picture of our publics and our leaders among them, it appears as though we have allowed the whole society of man to lose human innocence, to lose transparency, openness, where you are not afraid to face your own secret thoughts; and you are not ashamed if others see your own secret thoughts. In time, if you lose this core that G_d created us with, business life will be void of human life. The approach to troubling issues won't have the support of this life that G_d gave us to save us in every area of life. African American neighborhoods remain in business life in infancy, because the leadership, I mean our leadership, itself, is dead to man's original life that G_d gave us when He put us in the garden, or put our father, Adam, in the garden.

I got this saying from Christianity, from the Bible: *"Unless the children be reconciled with the father"*. Now I understand that it means the life, *"Unless the children's life be reconciled with the life of the father"*.[34] I know Christianity and perhaps, many Christians, they see this as reconciled with G_d. Yes, but, also, reconciled with Adam in his purity before he lost it to the seducer. 'Unless the children be reconciled in their life with the life of the father the whole earth will be cursed". And when I look at our world today on television and what leaders are talking about, the violence and the trouble in our world, it seems as though the whole world is under a curse.

What Holds Us Together as Citizens

Most of the world's religious traditions are now at home here in the United States of America. America's increasingly multi-religious reality challenges all of us to affirm the common covenant of our citizenship. Now let me explain that to you very quickly and easily. There are more religions coming into the United States. Within the last fifteen, or twenty years many different religions from Asia have come into the United States. So, the United States is getting more people who are citizens of the United States and they are alike as citizens, but they are different as worshipers of G_d. Their religions are different.

As a result, this makes it necessary for us to know what holds us together as citizens. It should be a part of our consciousness, a part of our efforts, to stay aware. It should be a responsibility and a part of our efforts to stay aware of important matters; and it should be part of our knowledge. We should have this in our knowledge, what we have in common with other American citizens, because that's what is going to bring us together. If we have that, also, in our religion, then we really have something going for us.

The common tie for citizens of the United States of America is basic in Islamic knowledge and teachings; that is, that there is a G_d Who has power over this United States. That is what one has to swear when he comes here to become a citizen. He raises his right hand, swears an allegiance to these United States, and he has to say, "One nation under G_d, with liberty and justice for all." He has to say that when he swears in. He has to recognize that this country is one nation under G_d, under Allah, and there is but one G_d. "We hold these truths to be self-evident that all men are created equal". That's our common tie.

When the Asian, or whoever comes here and becomes a citizen, he has to swear allegiance and he has to accept that in America all citizens are equal and entitled to the same basic rights. He has to accept that all American citizens recognize G_d as being the Power, not only over them in their church; but, also, over their country, the United States of America. They have to recognize that.

Liberty, the Freedom to Cultivate the Mind

This is what ties us to each other, that we all recognize that there is G_d over everything including our country; and we all recognize that we are equal in these United States in terms of the law, or the laws of the United States; that our citizenship gives us title to freedom and to liberty. Liberty goes farther than just being free. Liberty is the freedom to cultivate your mind, to get a good education; to have employment, to have business; to have ownership. Liberty, in the United States, goes so far as to give you the freedom to influence the course of government, to pick your leaders. If the majority of the people are not satisfied with their leaders, they can take them out of office by referendum. This is what ties us together. This is what we have in common. So, we should not forget that, because it should be common knowledge now. It should be a part of elementary school education that you know those things. Every child should learn that in school, know it, and appreciate it. This is what holds the citizens of the United States together.

A Buddhist is not like a Catholic. A Buddhist, in some respects, is not like a Muslim. A Muslim and a Hindu are not alike and there are many other religions, now, in this country that are not the same. We are not like each other. We don't speak one, common, religious language, but we speak one, common, language when it comes to human rights in these United States; and it respects the fact that there is a G_d over the United States.

No Interference with Religion

Another thing that we appreciate, today, as citizens in this American democracy is that this country cannot interfere with religion. It is in its laws that it cannot do that. It can't tell you how you are to be a Muslim. You have to go to your holy book, your guide, the Messenger of G_d, your Prophet, to know how to be a Muslim. This country can't tell you how to be a Muslim. But if you go against your own book and against your own Prophet, then this country can tell you, "Well, you say this is Islam. But we know it is not, because we have read your book, too." As a result, they will hold you to what you say you believe in. But they cannot make you change what you believe in. That's this country.

Good Because Allah Made You Good

Morals and manners are already imprinted in nature. You are not good because people teach you to be good. You are good because Allah made you good. You don't love good manners because people taught you that. You love good manners because Allah made you that way. But you had to be taught so that what's in you would have a brain to appreciate it and then you get some more of it. That's the way Allah is. Allah creates you, but He's not going to give you what He put in you to help you unless you, consciously, appreciate it. You have to consciously appreciate it. So, the society teaches you to appreciate something that G_d has already put in you and it starts to just express itself in you as good morals and good manners. You will even find this among people who have never been taught anything, who they call primitive, never having any civilization, education, or anything. They will have good morals and manners.

Chapter 4
Consultation and Consensus in Islam

There is no clergy in Islam. They speak of the Muslim clergy, but there is no such thing as a Muslim clergy. If we really want to know how the Muslim society is supposed to be, all we have to do is see what it was in Prophet Muhammed's day; see what he did; see how he formed the society. That's the way it should be now. If we could see it, we would say, "Oh boy, this is really not formal, not any particular class". Muhammed, the Prophet, did away with all that. He did away with those ritualistic formalities. He did away with class distinction. He forbade that they form these orders that separate an elitist group from the common people. That never happened. If you want to find the shuraa (consultative group, or body) today, how will you find it? I'm asking a question, right now. If you want to find the shuraa now, you go and locate a group of imams, or group of people who get together and they're men all the time, practically. They're men. They form the shuraa and they are supposed to be learned in Islam. That's number one. They're supposed to be learned in the religion, but are they supposed to be at such and such an address and in such and such city? No, they are supposed to be known by the community for their knowledge. They don't belong to any group. They belong to Islam.

He may be a doctor. He's got an office. He practices down the street from you, but he's known to have that great ability in Islam. People consult him and he's called when they want to meet to discuss things, because he has that knowledge. We're not supposed to be organized into two, four, or six men, or twenty men and they meet every so often, each month, or something. No, if the imams are meeting, they should have shuraa (consultation) for themselves and for their own interest. They're associated in a particular interest but that's not the shuraa. The shuraa is never in that narrow focus.

The shuraa will always be in the best minds and best character in the Muslim community and it will include females. Who can say a woman with a great mind like the lady, Aisha (the wife of Prophet Muhammed), who can say that she wasn't a part of the shuraa? So, the real shuraa will, also, include females.

The Common Essence of All People

To get where Allah wants us to go we have to become as Adam when G_d made him. And if you understand him from the Bible and from Qur'an, he is a single soul; but he is a figure representing all people; for he is the common essence of all people; their common essence that has been created and directed by G_d. The Bible speaks of Adam in the singular and in the plural concept, not just a single concept; but a concept that is inclusive of all people, all mankind. The Qur'an speaks of him in the same way. He fell from the high position given to him by his Creator, when he listened to the suggestions of the enemy of all mankind, the devil, Satan (Shaitan/Shaytan), Lucifer. This is Qur'an.

What Is the Enemy of Man?

He is given all of these names, but the most important name you should remember is that he is the enemy of all mankind. So, what is he? Is he a man? No, he is the enemy of man. He is not a man. So, what is he? He is fire. That is what He says to G_d, in the Qur'an. He said, *"I will not accept, or submit to this ruler You want to put in the earth; a mortal You made from the earth. You made me better than he! You made me of fire!"*[35] And to really understand him, he is a fire that really gives off no smoke, meaning he has nothing to repent. In his own mind, he thinks he has nothing to repent. "So, why should I burn and give off smoke? I burn, but I do not give off anything. I do not give up anything"; a self-contained fire burning on its own will power.

Look in Your Own Heart

He is really a big braggart, arrogant, boastful and thinks he has every right to decide matters for the whole of mankind on this earth, arbitrarily, and he does not have to consult anybody. Where are you looking for him? Are you looking for him somewhere? I can imagine somebody looking around for him. But the first place to look is in your own heart. That is where he wants to get. Anywhere you find a convincing picture resembling what I just told you of the descriptions of Satan, be careful. Don't get involved there acting arbitrarily, being boastful, thinking yourself more important than everything else and making decisions without consulting decent persons who qualify to contribute to whatever plan we have for our communities, or for our world.

Human Community Cannot Live Alone Anymore

Include others when you want to plan the future for mankind, or the future for your community. Consult others. In Islam, the believers are those who conduct their affairs by shuraa baynahum (consulting with each other). They conduct their affairs by consulting those of us who qualify as people of good character, knowledge, and experience. We consult them. We put our heads together. We don't go alone. So, this is the future and this is the time for that future; a time not just for leaders, but for nations to put their heads together and agree that we cannot go it alone; a time to put their heads together when they want to plan life on this earth for a community of people, because the human community cannot live alone anymore.

Creation of the Individual Requisitions the Life of Society

In the practice of Islam, the obligated prayers performed five times a day at established times are called, the fard prayers and are group prayers. And the group can be as small as three persons, three mature persons. Well, in your family, it can be you and two of your children. It doesn't have to be mature persons. But in the public, or in our public, in the Muslim public, like at the masjid (mosque), or someplace where we're doing the prayer, I think it should be at least three mature persons; not just the imam and two children following behind him. That's not the public picture we want. That's not the message we want to send to society. So, we need at least three mature persons for the group prayer in public done outside of the private home.

In Final Analysis Society More Important Than Individual

What does this say? The three should be the society. Three in this focus represent the needs of the society, or should have a reference to the nature and need of society; the three. The society then, is more important in the final analysis than the individual. That is to say, the needs of the society are more binding on us than the individual needs. I said, in the final analysis. Why did I put it that way? Because in the beginning of society, in the beginning of the creation of society, the individual is where the importance lies, because the creation of the individual requisitions the life of society. Is that understood? Yes, it is the creation of the individual that requisitions the life of society. But when the society begins to group, when three mature persons come together, then it's no longer about the individual. Two represents the individual. Three represent the goal for the individual, or the aim for the individual's life; and the aim, or the goal is to be realized in the external, or the outer environment; the objective world.

The Development and Growth of Life a Group Project

So, we group to grow in the environment, to grow into the plan that G_d has made for our life. The plan is bigger than we are when we are made, or created; a big plan. We have to fill the capacity, or the rooms that Allah has made for our life and the rooms are so many and so big (i.e., the environment). So, the job, or the work, the responsibility to develop and grow so that our life occupies all the rooms that G_d created for that life to live in and occupy, is a group responsibility. It is not an individual responsibility. The human being can't do it with just an individual. No one leader can do it. No one human being, no one leader can do it. It takes the whole group. It's a group project.

"The Hand of G_d Is on the Collective Body"

So, it was impossible for Allah to reveal to any one man the plan for our social destiny and that one man lead us into that destiny by himself; not even with revelation; not even with his sunnah (lifestyle, i.e., sayings and traditions) can he do it! He has to invite the participation of the excellent men and women, or persons, in his environment and together they work. That's shuraa. Shuraa is binding, even on the Prophet. So, the most important elements for establishing the Islamic community are the Word of G_d, the Qur'an, the sunnah (Muhammed's life of living the Qur'an) and shuraa (consultation). You can't have it without shuraa. You can have the Qur'an and have the sunnah, but you still can't have it without shuraa, without consultation. In fact, it is Qur'an and sunnah to have shuraa. Thus, we have to have that third dimension there, or third element working in our lives for us, the shuraa.

Allah says indirectly, but says, directly, through Muhammed, the Prophet (the prayers and peace be upon him) in hadith, "Yadullah ala jama'". Literally, it says that, "The Hand of G_d is on the group, on the collective body"; that is, the society. "The Hand of G_d is on the collective body". But this, "Hand", is understood, by the scholars to mean that G_d obligates the collective body. Now, we know He obligates individuals, but this is a bigger importance and it's expressed that way that ultimately and more importantly,

G_d obligates the collective body. It means His control is on the collective body. What is His control for? His control is to protect His plan for the collective body. That is what His control is for, to protect His plan in and for the collective body. So, how are we going to be progressed? We're going to be progressed because of the collective body accepting responsibility for that. [36]

Islam Is a Republic

Therefore, that would say that Islam is a republic, wouldn't it? Islam is a republic. It is a society that holds its public responsible for its state. By state, here, I mean the condition for its future, although we know Allah always is the Protector. He is the Guarantor. He guarantees us the future, but the onus falls on us to be responsible for our own life and our own lives. So, it says that the Islamic society is a society that holds its citizens responsible, or sees them as qualified to carry responsibility for the state of the society and for its future. This is a true republic, the Islamic republic.

We know in the case of Muhammed, the Prophet, when he, himself, made appointments, he sought the support of the most qualified ones in terms of good character and knowledge. He sought support for the person that he would appoint. Many times, he didn't appoint persons at all. Most of the time, he left it to the people to appoint persons to represent them in positions of authority.

Islam Is a Democracy

Therefore, Islam, for want of a better word, is a democracy. However, the expression in Islam is, "Shuraa baynahum"; that is, they consult one another. They have mutual consultation, respecting each other as equals; equally qualified to give advice, to contribute to decision-making. "Baynahum", means just that, mutual. I offer my advice and, also, another person has the same right; and he offers his advice and then we look at all of it and come to conclusion based upon the strongest support that we have from those qualified persons. This is the main description, I would say, of democracy in Islam. This is the main focus for our understanding and perception of how we should manage our affairs. G_d says, in the Qur'an, *"The believers manage their affairs by shuraa baynahum"*.[37]

Democracy and Shuraa Have Same Meaning

Islam wants freedom, too. Islam wants respect for the opinions, the intelligence, of all of us. And if we have differences with each other, we should speak up and we should work to get our point over. If you're convinced that your point is right, correct, work to get it over. This is Islam. This is democracy, Islamic democracy. This is shuraa. So, the word we have is, "Shuraa" and not, "Democracy". But, it's the same. What democracy means to American society with maybe slight differences, shuraa means for Muslims. But for Muslims the whole expression is, "Shuraa baynahum, consulting each other"; the best of minds and character consulting each other. And when there's a matter that the community has to address that may affect the community in a serious way, those persons of the best mind and the best character should sit down and consult with each other.

Concerns and Demands of Women Should be Included

Therefore, we should include the women; not that you should mix the two. We don't mix the two, but we accept, we admit the concerns of women and the demands of women. It's in the Qur'an. *"Al-Jaadillah, the Woman Who Complains"*.[38] Yes, it's there representing all women that may have complaints. And it was the way of the leadership, in the time of our Prophet and after him, under the great leaders, the khalifahs and companions of Prophet Muhammed, may G_d be pleased with them. It was the habit of the men to not only listen to women, but, sometimes, to hint that, "We need your advice", or, to ask their advice. They would, also, ask for their advice and they could speak out in the public.

You know, in the past Church leaders (it's very unpopular now) would say, "The woman's voice should not be heard in the public". In the public, her voice should not be heard. Maybe in the congregation, but in the public, she should speak quietly and privately. But this was not the case in the time of our Prophet, or after. The women were encouraged to speak up and they did. And we have in the history, on record, women questioning great rulers, the great rulers; questioning them in a public place and getting them to acknowledge the issue, or the complaint and to address it. We have on record where the ruler has admitted that he was in error, because a woman brought him to account.

Our Life Is the Word of G_d, a Conscious Life

This is Islam. This is shuraa baynahum. This is the way of Islam. So, in this America the only thing that can hurt us, now, this community, this association of Muslims that I'm with, is old, bad, habits from the past; and mostly, from the Nation of Islam; those bad habits from the Nation of Islam so deeply ingrained in some of us that we're still marching to the cadence of the old captains and lieutenants. We're still marching to that cadence. We have to break from those habits and live, consciously. That's the only way to live. A Muslim's life is a conscious life. That's another point. The life is the Word of G_d, the real life and that life is a conscious life. We have to live consciously; live consciously, not by habits. Don't live by habits. Live consciously. Living consciously improves habit. This is the meaning of the greeting (at the end of the Islamic prayer) to the right, "As-salaamu 'alaikum wa rahmatullah" and then greeting to the left, "As-salaamu 'alaikum wa rahmatullah"; translated, "The peace be upon you and the Mercy of G_d". If you establish the conscious life, in peace, it will take care of the unconscious life; then we turn to the left. Where is it going to come from? What's going to improve my life's habits? What's going to improve my unconscious behavior? It's my conscious behavior. If you want to strengthen the behavior in a person, build their conscious behavior and that will strengthen their unconscious behavior. And after a while the conscious behavior becomes the unconscious behavior. That is how it works.

Now, the sincere, faithful, believers, all should go and form teams. The better minds, all of them, are obligated to form teams to work with the shuraa, to work with the leadership. They should form teams and let it come down from the shuraa and the leadership, and let the work be spread out all over the community throughout these United States. What are we working on? We're working on applying the five principles of Islam to get the benefits G_d intends for us, for our community life on this earth. That's the answer and that's Islam!

Putting Healing Medicine into the Public Life

When I'm speaking to the public, the American public, I am imparting to them something of the purity of the essence of Islam as much as I think they can take. So, what are we doing? We're fighting the germs that fight against the Muslim life that are in the public life. So, we're putting the healing medicine into the public life so that the public will be healed of those germs that threaten our life, to accommodate more expression of our life in this world. This is a masterful job that G_d has given me! A masterful job to open up this world so it accommodates our growth, and at the same time, we're extending the Mercy of G_d to them, because they need a healing; and if they get good medicine, they will recognize good medicine. As a result, those that don't need what we're passing to them they applaud it. "Oh, we like this man they've got! We like this leader that they've got! He's a good man!" Praise be to G_d! So, Muhammed (his life and example) is not only a mercy to the Muslims. He is a mercy to all the worlds. In reality, that's how I live. I live as his follower so that my life will be not only a mercy to my family and my community, but be a mercy to the worlds. Actually, that's how each of us should live.

Satan Thinks He's Helping G_d

In Islam, Satan is seen as the enemy of man: "Aduwan nas, the enemy of humanity, the enemy of all humans".[39] It doesn't say the enemy of G_d, but you know he's is G_d's enemy, too. However, he's not G_d's enemy in his own mind. That's what you have to understand. This is an entity who is so captivated, so possessed by his own mind and thinking that he can't see that he's really the enemy of G_d. This is not talking about something that is supernatural. This not talking about something that is a supernatural being in another reality. This is talking about something that is in the real world of human beings. So, he can't accept that he's wrong, or that he's against G_d. He thinks he's with G_d.

So, the devil (Satan) can be in the Church. He can be in the Mosque. The devil (Satan) can be in the Synagogue. Satan can be in the government of the United States. Satan can be in Israel in the government there. Satan can be in Saudi Arabia in the government, because Satan doesn't even know he's working against G_d. He's so possessed by his own thinking he doesn't even know he's working against G_d. He thinks he's working for G_d. So, he says, "This is not going to work. What you have isn't going to work for you. I care about you more than you care about yourself and I'm going to show you that what you are doing, here, is not going to work. I'm going to prove that this creature that You're giving all this love and attention to, and respect to, trusting him with responsibility in the earth for forming the order of life down here, I'm going to prove to You that he's not worthy!"

A Democracy Inviting All to Come to the Top

How does the Bible say this? *"Seven eyes went out to condemn man, to disprove, to prove man unworthy of the great station that G_d assigned for man. And seven eyes went out to prove him"*.[40] So, these are the two positions and the two forces that are working in man's world. One is working to prove him unfit to be on his own, to be free with his own mind, to develop into a society where responsibility for that society is trusted to many and not one. The other is working so that man is free to have his republic, his democracy; whatever term we may use to try to give you a picture of what we're talking about. This is in the nature of man, isn't it? It is in the nature of man to not trust others if he thinks himself superior to them; and because that disposition is taken dictatorships form.

And then, there is, also, in man the feeling and sensitivity, the disposition that, "Even though they are not my equal in knowledge, they are made just like I am, with the same possibilities for them that I have for myself. Though I am superior to them, now, and they are depending on me and they need me like children need their parents, I know they have the same potential, the same capacity, etc., that I have. I want to see them grow up to my level. I want to see these babies become grownups. So, I'm going to form a democracy, a republic, that will invite all of them to come to the top"; and many of them will come, in time. You see, that's the disposition that respects the creation of human beings, or respects what G_d made and what G_d wants for the human being He made. So that, maybe put in language is the, "Seven eyes that go out to approve man", in that wonderful station given him by his Creator.

The Best of Themselves

I mentioned that even in Arabia, as ignorant and as savage and backwards as it was there, Muhammed was not like that. There were his friends who were not like that and some writers say that these people, before Islam, were called, "Hunafaa" (upright, not worshiping idols). And when Allah referred to people by that name, He was referring to them; and He was referring to Abraham, directly; but, also, to Muhammed, to his friends and to many others; although they represented a small percentage of the population of the Arabs, who didn't believe in idols, didn't worship idols, and who had excellent human character and manners before Islam came. They rejected the way of the world on the strength of what they believed about the excellence of their human person; and they didn't even refer to themselves as human; just to the person, the man, the excellence of the creation of man; or the makeup of man. They didn't even think about man as a creation, in fact, before Islam came to them. Islam had to tell the Arabs that man was created by G_d. They didn't know that. That wasn't their thinking. But they believed that this body and this being is superior to animals; therefore, your behavior should be superior to animal behavior. They just followed logic. They followed good, rational, human, common sense logic. And their conclusion was that they should present the best of themselves, always, and not the worst of themselves.

Every Man Inherently Honorable

So, that was proof, wasn't it? That was proof that the man that G_d created, the human being that G_d created, was created in excellence, was created in great form, was excellent, inherently. When G_d says, *"Qad karamna kulli bani Adam, certainly We made honorable every child of Adam"*, or, *"every son of Adam"*; when G_d says that, you who are on the college level, you should know that G_d is saying that every human person is, inherently, honorable. That's what G_d is saying.[41]

Now, if you are a fifth grader and you didn't get any more education and you haven't tried to study on your own, then I don't expect for you to come up with that conclusion. But any of you in college and above, when you hear that expression, you should come to conclusion G_d is saying that we are honorable by virtue of our own constitution and creation, or our make-up; made superior to animals and other creatures; and that none of us are different in the original constitution of ourselves, how we are originally made. We don't even have to bring G_d into the picture as to how we were originally made. The earth made us. The sun made us; whatever, made us.

In our original constitution, we are superior to all those other creatures and we are not inferior to any other in our original constitution. No! In no way are we inferior to any other human being in our original constitution. We have a brain, the same human brain that all others have. We have eyes. We have these human faculties that enable us to perform intelligently, morally, and justly, etc.

All of us are equipped that way. That's why when they opened up an opportunity, blacks proved themselves just as capable of fulfilling those positions as whites did. In fact, in many positions, they excelled. Look at Colin Powell. We didn't know we had a general like that, back there, when they said you couldn't rise that high. But they gave him opportunity and that man became the chief of staff for the Pentagon; Colin Powell, a black man, an African

American. Consequently, President George Bush Jr. appointed an African American soldier, a military man, the great general, Colin Powell, to the position of Secretary of State.

Rights by Virtue of Your Own Creation

So, we all are created equal, have the same essence and that's in the Constitution of these United States: "We hold these truths to be self-evident that all men are created equal and endowed with inalienable rights"; some say, "unalienable rights". It means rights that can't be taken away from you because they are yours by virtue of your own creation. They belong to you. As a created thing, or as a made thing, they belong to you. They are endowed with inalienable rights, "And among these, life, liberty and the pursuit of happiness"; endowed by their Creator, recognizing G_d, also. That's a very important to know. "Endowed by their Creator with inalienable rights and among these life, liberty and pursuit of happiness."

So, you have equal essence. That's what the Constitution is saying and that's what the Qur'an said centuries before the Constitution of the United States; more than a thousand years before the United States came into existence. The Qur'an, G_d's Word in Qur'an, was saying that you have inalienable rights given to you in your creation by your Creator. By virtue of your creation you have these inalienable rights. The Founding Fathers elaborated on that: "Among these are life, liberty and the pursuit of happiness..."

Chapter 5

Islam and American Democracy

When you read the first chapter of the Qur'an, Al-Fatiha, and come to understand it, you will know that Al-Fatiha helps us to understand why the story of the people of 'Ad and any other people are in the Qur'an. It is because Allah (G_d) is Lord of all people. He cares about all the worlds and they could not have any history without G_d; and we could not have history. We could not have this nation, nor have our form of government without revelation.[42]

The Language of the Founding Fathers Closest to Qur'an

The closest ideology for authority over the people, providing for them an ideology, or a political ideology to govern their lives as a governmental order, or a political order; the closest to what Allah planned in Scripture before Qur'an and in Qur'an, is what we find in the language of the Founding Fathers for our Constitution in this society that we have; and I can prove it. We could not have this beautiful form of government we have, if the Qur'an had not come. There was no government like we have in these United States before the Qur'an.

The Christians were not able to establish a government like this before the Qur'an. It was the Qur'an that guided the Founding Fathers to conceive what was in their own book, the Bible; and they used the Qur'an to arrive at the logic supporting this philosophy called, American democracy. It is said that the first president, George Washington, had knowledge of Qur'an. James Madison was known to have spoken highly of the Qur'an, Muhammed, the Prophet, and Islam; also, Thomas Jefferson, the main framer of the Constitution. So, those people back there who formed this idea we call, American democracy, were acquainted with Muhammed, the Prophet, and the Qur'an, and they, definitely, were inspired by him and guided by his knowledge that G_d gave him to form the ideas supporting the Constitution of the United States of America. This I'm convinced of. I have no doubts at all about that. I know that.

Islam is a religion for the salvation of the individual, for the spiritual good life of the individual person that situates them, spiritually, to enjoy the fullness of life, the fullness of family life; business life, or real life; the whole life. But, this religion does this for the community, too. It does it with the individual in the focus; but then the religion, also, focuses on community life. And it has in its focus, as its community goal, the global community, the whole world. So, our religion is not just a religion for personal salvation. Our religion (Islam) is a religion that's in competition with world ideologies; and its purpose is to advance the good message, advance the good life so the whole globe will one day at least have an opportunity to have it; say, "Yes", or, "No" to it.

Call to the Path of G_d

Our dawah (call, or invitation) can never be limited to ourselves, or, to our nation. Our dawah it must be open and extended, opened for the world to see it and accept it, or choose it if they want to; and it must be extended to them as an invitation to Islam, the invitation to be a Muslim, to accept the religion of Islam. This is our dawah. So, first, we should know if this is the dawah. Dawah, also, has another meaning. It means, to call, because G_d says, *"Call to the path of G_d"*.[43] So, the dawah is an invitation. Dawah is a call. We invite and we call people to the way of G_d, in Islam; and the call is to go out from us to our nearest relatives, our friends, our neighbors, the whole world, eventually. This is where it's going.

Islam started in Saudi Arabia, in Mecca, went to Madinah, in Saudi Arabia, what is called, Saudi Arabia. It wasn't called, Saudi Arabia, at that time and much of the world was not called what it's called now. It went from there to Abyssinia, Africa, what is called, Ethiopia now. And it, also, went to Persia, what is called Iran now. It went to Syria and it went to all of the Middle Eastern countries. It went to Europe, to Spain, and, eventually, India, far East India. It went to India and to China and, eventually, to Russia.

Islam Competes with Democracy

Islam is a global ideology for global reform to bring about global change, global reformation, so that man will come back to the original nature that G_d gave him, when He put him in the garden. This is our religion. So, we look at it from that viewpoint, stand point. We have looked at our religion from that standpoint. What is the religion for me and for the world? It is personal salvation; but it is, also, salvation for the community of man on this earth. Therefore, it is in competition with other ideologies that claim that they serve the good and the good future of the whole people on this earth.

Democracy, Western democracy, has that claim and Western democracy is pushing itself to advance itself all over the world, so that it will convert all nations to the democratic idea of the Founding Fathers. They are doing that, quietly, and they are doing that, loudly. So, Islam is, also, in competition with Western democracy, because Islam promises the individual, too, that G_d is going to bring you into the best life, the ideal life, and the ideal society. This is Islam. Both democracy, Western democracy, and the Islamic ummah (community), both of these ideas, or these ideologies, they are responding to the oppressors of our humanity. Thus, if you understand, if you read carefully the Qur'an and if you study as a student and G_d blesses you, guides you, has mercy and guides you in the way, you will find that Islam is addressing notions of human worth that discredited human worth.

The Bible addresses it, too, the notions, the popular notions, in the world of human worth that discredited human worth. So, Islam comes back and G_d addresses it in Qur'an, the language of Qur'an and with the model, person Muhammed (peace be upon him), to tell us, but also, to show us that this human being that they very lowly esteemed is much more than they estimated this human being to be.

Good News for the Human Family

The old idea was that if you're not educated, if you don't get an education, there's no hope for you; that you will stay an animal; that you will stay on the animal level, unless you get education; and education was their idea. The illumination of the mind, it was their idea of education. So, the fortunate ones were able to get knowledge and because of getting knowledge others didn't have, they got advantages over others. They became the masters, the rulers over others. The old world, the ancient world and much of medieval world that had not changed, they considered the human being in his human reality to be a cheap creation; something to be treated just like you treat an animal. And many times, they treated human beings as their human subjects worse than they treated their animals; not just blacks. Whites and everybody were treated like that; women, men, whites, everybody.

Islam and Democracy Place High Value on the Human Being

Islam is addressing that. So, Islam wants to bring the good news to the human family, especially, to the oppressed of the human family that, "This world's leaders, the oppressors of your humanity, they have evaluated you and have estimated you to be something very mean, low and cheap in your reality; but G_d has not. G_d, who created you respects you, and He highly values, or He places a high value on you, on your real human worth". So, American democracy and Islam come into the world to challenge this idea in the power structure of the world that the human being in his true human state, is not much to be respected. Frederick Douglas said, "They claim Christ Jesus", peace be on G_d's servant. And Frederick Douglas said, "And you claim your democracy to be the best democracy." He said, "But your behavior is such that it would shame a nation of savages." Those are the words of the great teacher, educator, liberator, and freedom fighter, Frederick Douglas.[44]

Keep your mind on this picture, now, and look in the Old Testament and see how the Jews were mistreated and see what G_d had to do as an obligation. Now, tell me, looking at that picture of the Jews in their treatment and how they were under a hard task master, a bad-natured Pharaoh, and how he had subjected them to raw, material, performances and would not permit them to develop their intellect and their spirituality; not under him. With him observing it, if he saw it, he would punish them for it. And look at African Americans, coming up, how they were in the South during the days of slavery in these United States, called, "A peculiar institution of slavery". This is what the historians say about it, the peculiar institution of slavery, meaning that there was not another like it in the history of man.

G_d Obligated to Help Us

So, looking at all this, now, and understanding that the G_d Who created blacks for the life, is seeing them held back from it by a people who claimed to be the leaders of democracy, the leaders of the best order of society for man; and claiming, also, to be followers of Christ Jesus, the righteous, a Word from G_d; Jesus Christ, peace be on him. Tell me what do you think G_d will be obligated to do? He is obligated to take over and work for those that have been oppressed. He is obligated to do that. People are being held back from what He created them to be and they are holding them back in His name. G_d says, if you publish something in His name, you obligate Him. That is Scripture.

If you publish something in His name, G_d says you obligate Him. Now, I'm speaking of what the white man did saying that they represented the society of Christ Jesus; that they were authorized by G_d's Word to do these things, to have the society as they had it; a terrible shame in the eyes of any intelligent man, or beast. An animal would cry, if they could understand the situation. I'm sure a lot of dogs did cry looking at the condition of the slaves, the way they were treated. I can see them and hear them, now. I'm sure they did it; and a horse, too, in his own way, a mule and all of them. I bet you a chicken, too, saw us in our misery and that rooster gave a mournful crowing.

All the Way to Where He wants Them to Go as Human Beings

Every living thing pitied black people in the state that we were in, pitied the treatment that we were getting from another so-called human brother. Now, what do you think G_d is going to do? So, is it a big thing that I tell you G_d has guided Imam W. Deen Mohammed and gave Imam W. Deen Mohammed what he needs to take those who will follow him all the way to where G_d wants them to go as human beings? And Muslims in this association are absolutely hurting their own selves, cutting their own selves out of the blessings, when they want what some other person is saying as a leader of Islam over what I tell them. And you go to their book and put down the book that I give you. You go to their book and get their language and put down the language that I give you. You are under a curse! G_d has cut you out of the blessings and that is just plain truth that I'm giving you as a brother and a friend; because I forgive you. This isn't personal. I am not in this for myself. No, indeed! So, I'm hurt when you turn me down. I am hurt for you when you turn me down; not for myself. No, indeed! That's what we should expect; no less than that we should expect.

At this point, I want to refer to Chapter 52 of the Qur'an, where G_d says: *"Now await in patience the command of your Lord, for verily you are in Our eyes."* This is directed to Prophet Muhammed, himself, but it includes all of us. G_d is aware of all of us and He sees all of us all the time. The verse continues, *"And celebrate the praises of your Lord while you stand forth."* I am giving you the translation in English that is in the Qur'an, translated by Abdullah Yusuf Ali, the one that we recommend. Although you can read any translation of the Qur'an into English you like, that is the one we recommend.[45]

The Standing Position, the Highest Position for Man

Repeating, *"And celebrate the praises of your Lord while you stand forth."* Standing, that is what we want to focus our minds on right now. Every prayer in Islam begins with standing. We are given the signal when to stand and the signal says, "Now, for sure, it's time to stand for prayer". In Arabic, it is, "Qad qaamatis salat." The Arabic word, "Qad", means, "For sure, right now". And we stand for prayer and in that position, we praise G_d. We say, *"Bismillahir rahmaanir raheem. Al hamdu lillahi rabbil 'alameen. With G_d's Name, the Merciful Benefactor, the Merciful Redeemer. All Praises are for G_d, the Lord of all systems of Knowledge".*[46] In that position, we praise G_d. That is the beginning of our utterance, when we make the stand. In fact, following some, you don't hear, "Bismillah". In fact, the majority, you don't hear them say it out loud. They say it in their heart. They begin the recital with, *"Al hamdu lillaahi rabbil 'alameen."*[47] And it is in the sayings of the Prophet, Muhammed, that that expression holds up the sky.

When you are standing, your stature, or your form, is as high as it can be. You don't pray on your tiptoes. When you stand on your feet, you are standing as high as you can, because you are supposed to stand erect in prayer; not bent over, not sloughed, but standing erect. We praise G_d in that position. That is the highest position of man, the standing position. And when he is standing, he feels his power and he feels his dignity. When he feels his dignity, he wants to stand erect, straight up. This is the position that you take that can get you in trouble, if you are not praising G_d. So, in that position, the first thing you say is, *"Al hamdu lillaahi rabbil 'alameen, the praise is for G_d, the Lord of all the worlds"*, while you stand forth. And in the Judgment, will you sit for Judgment, or will you stand for Judgment? We stand for Judgment. The Judgment Day is called, The Day of Standing and in Qur'anic Arabic, it is pronounced, "Yaumal Qiyaamah." The English translation for Jumah Prayer, Salatul Jumah, is, "The Day of Assembly" and that is what we do. We assemble and we call it Jumah Prayer. It means the prayer done by the collective group members, all together.[48]

"And You Are a Free Man in the City"

Let us now change the focus from man in the standing position to the Prophet, Muhammed, as a model for us. And this time, we want to speak of the Prophet in connection with what G_d says in the chapter of the Qur'an called, "The City, Al Balad" and verse 2 of that chapter.[49] I want to share with you, also, from Abdullah Yusuf Ali's commentary on that verse, footnote #6131. Allah says of Muhammed, the Prophet, *"And you are a freeman of this city."* Let us see in the notes what Abdullah Yusuf Ali says about this. He says, "The word for, 'free man', is, 'Hill', or 'Hilun'. When you read it, you have, "Hilun". The pronunciation changes following the rules of Qur'anic reading. It is, *"Hilum bi haadhaal balad."* In these times that we are living in, especially as influenced by democracy in America, many of Muslim scholars and teachers do not want us to say, "Freeman", and they say it does not say, "Freeman." But Abdullah Yusuf Ali is no ignorant translator. He is well-respected in Mecca, Egypt, all the powerful Islamic centers of knowledge. So, if he says, "Freeman", let us see why he says, "Freeman".

He says it means Prophet Muhammed is, "An inhabitant. G_d is saying he is an inhabitant of that town, a man with lawful rights; a man free from such obligations as would attach to a stranger to the city; a free man, in a wider sense than the technical sense to which the word is restricted in modern usage. The Prophet should have been honored in his native city. He was, actually, being persecuted. He should have been loved as a parent loves a child. Actually, his life was being sought and those who believed in him were under a ban"; that is, they were under restrictions. They could not have the privileges that the other free citizens had. They called a boycott against Prophet Muhammed and his followers. Some of you are familiar with this history of Prophet Muhammed. But time was to show that he was to return triumphant to his native city, after having made Madinah sacred by his life and work.[50]

Free Citizens of the United States

Now, we are free citizens in the United States. In what sense, or by what reference are we free citizens of the United States? You have to go back to the legislation. You have to go back to the process of freedom in the United States, the growth and development of freedom for the people of the United States; because when they first formed the language of the Constitution for this nation, they said that we are free by virtue of the fact that all human beings are created the same; or have the same common worth. We all have our five senses. We all have our freedom to question things. We all have this same great brain that G_d gave only to humans, not to animals. And since we all have the same life form and the same brain, the founders, or writers for framing the language of the Constitution established that all citizens are equal and are due the same rights accorded to anyone else; and those rights can never be taken from us by political power, or government. Those rights are inherent rights, meaning that they came with our form that G_d gave us. That's clear, isn't it?

We are free citizens. That was not the freedom given to us in the wilds. This freedom that we are talking about that is given to us and protected by the Constitution of these United States and the good people, it was given to us under a government body that was planning for our future generations to come. That is how it came to us and it has been protected by the people through their legislation.

Political and Social Leaders Before the Prophet

So, when we say of Muhammed, the Prophet, that G_d said of him he is, *"A freeman of this town"*, we are saying it with respect for civilized order, or civilized establishments, governments. And the Meccans, though they were behaving not as civilized people, they had established laws long before the generation of Muhammed, the Prophet. Those laws had been established for the Arabs and they had social reform teachers before Muhammed, the Prophet and they had gone astray. I'm not talking about Prophet Ibraheem (Abraham). They had social reform teachers who were not Messengers, or Prophets of G_d to help them come to some sense of social order and government. And they were not behaving even with respect for their high leaders, those political and social guides who were before, or generations before the time of Muhammed, the Prophet. So, they had not only gone astray. They did not know Abraham's way. That had been completely lost. But they had not only lost that. They had, also, lost the better teachings for social order and government that they had received in previous times.

Qur'an to be Read in a Context

So, this statement is not one that you can just hear and deal with nothing but words. In fact, I don't know any statement in the

Qur'an that you can treat that way. You can't just read what is in the Qur'an and deal with it as though it is nothing but words. No, those words have a social context, a spiritual context, and a political context. They have a context. They fit in a particular focus, a particular framework and they, also, have a time context, a time framework, etc. That is not all there is to it.

Accordingly, don't think you can just read something in the Qur'an and now you are a Ph. D and you want to question everybody based upon what you know. Do you want to question everybody based upon what you know? You can't handle the Qur'an like that. Please, that is not the way to handle any respected book. If you give me a statement from any respected book, you have to respect what that book requires of the reader. The same is for the Qur'an. There is no difference. It is even more so, because it is a sacred book with the words directly from G_d, Himself.

The worst thing we can do is allow our prejudice as people who are not satisfied with Arabs, or not satisfied with the American government, to go to the extreme. That is the worst thing we can do and we have those two extremes. One of the extremes we have is those who have prejudices against Arabs and you would like to do away with the tradition of Muhammed and make your own Islam. Then we have the other extreme where we have those who just hate to give credit to the United States of America. They don't want to acknowledge the United States for the credit that it is due among us, African Americans and, also, outside. That extreme, too, blinds your eyes to the guidance of G_d in the Qur'an. You cannot expect to get the pure, clear message of G_d that is for us in the Qur'an, if you are going to have prejudices that are unjust.

Turning to Something That Is Supernatural

Unfortunately, the management of our life has become too troublesome for us. When it comes to the public life, it is too troublesome for us. We can't handle it. We can't turn people around. We can't speak to them and they respect what we are saying. So, what happens? We who want to keep the valuable human life, we turn to the supernatural. Those who are already in a religion, like Christians and Jews, we turn to the strength of our religion.

For Muslims, it is the same. We turn to the strength of our religion. But sometimes, right direction is so confused, even in our religion. We say, "I just can't find any help. I've been reading this Bible and I can't find any help." This may surprise you to hear. "I have been reading this Qur'an and I just can't find help." I have heard it. Thus, we turn to the supernatural by some name and, sometimes, by no name saying, "I don't know what His name is. I know that there is a G_d, but I just can't be comfortable anymore with what I have been following."

As a result, you go on your own still believing in the supernatural. That means something that is not subjected to the fate that we are subjected to, or that natural life is subjected to; Something that does not get sick; Something that does not get confused; Something that does not get worried, or something like that; or Something that does not breakdown when difficulty comes. We, therefore, turn to Something that we say is supernatural. "I know there is a Cause behind all this. I know there is Something that brought all of this world about and Something that caused me to be here, etc."

We turn to our own imagination and to our own concerns and we say, "I just can't follow what I have been given before. It is not helping." Consequently, I have come to believe, if you remain sincere, G_d comes to you. You may ask, "Does G_d comes to us, too?" Yes, He does! Just hold on!

Establishing One's Life in the Context of Community

The people of the book had been told, *"No one has ascended into heaven, except he who was already in heaven"*. That is the Bible.[51] Now, understand that this was left with the people of book; also, they were given a picture of Adam, or an idea, or concept of Adam, the first human being, as the forebear of all humanity; the first human being, the beginning of humanity on the earth. He wasn't born of man's flesh. Adam was created. It is important to comprehend what is given in the Qur'an regarding necessary steps that have to be taken to establish one's life in the context of community, or of community life. The natural progression for our spirit, our soul, and our human content that G_d created begins with us having a desire inside of ourselves to establish ourselves spiritually; but we don't think in those terms. Actually, the desire is to establish our soul, but we don't think in those terms.

We just know we need to make something better inside of us. When our spirit and thinking when we're trying to manage our life becomes too troublesome for us, we turn to the supernatural. Even if we keep the religion, we still turn to the supernatural. You are turning to Him on your own. You don't have the preacher telling you how to turn to Him though you go to church. You don't have the rabbi of the synagogue, or the imam of the mosque telling you how to deal with this; though you go to the temple, or the mosque. It has become a private affair. You want to work this out between you and your Lord.

"He Who Created Me Guides Me"

In the Qur'an, when the mighty Pharaoh was trying to break the spirit of the Prophet who was defying him, he warned the Prophet that, "I could cut you a loose, now; and if I banish you, or cut you a loose, what are you going to do? How are you going to make it in life?" The Prophet said to Pharaoh, *"The One Who created me will guide me"*.[52] Do you notice how he put that? What is he saying? "I am guided through my own human creation". There is that Qibla, again! "I am guided through my own human creation".

That is what he is telling the oppressive Pharaoh. He didn't have G_d with him and Pharaoh didn't say, "Are you talking about that One Who is standing by you there?" No. There was nobody around; nobody but him is talking to Pharaoh. However, he knew that he didn't get his creation on his own and that he nor any other human being could design his creation and make it come into existence. Therefore, he was saying that, "Whoever, Whatever, gave me this marvelous creation left enough guidance in my own creation for me to follow to make it on my own. Pharaoh, I don't need you!"

Stand Up in Your Own Soul

We have to establish ourselves in our own soul. You have to be able to stand up in your own soul. If you can't face your soul without falling down, then you need to get help. And there is help in the Qur'an and in the life of Muhammed, the model of human excellence for all of us. Muhammed, the Prophet, when he was called by Allah to be the last Prophet, he was seeking Allah. He was seeking answers. He was troubled by the confusion of the world, at that time, and the condition of people burdened his heart. So, he sought Allah. He went to find the Supernatural. He had already lived a lifetime among his people, the life G_d established Muhammed in. He did not lose his original creation that G_d gave him for the first time, the Adam nature, the original man. He was still in that original nature. He did not come out of it and he was forty years old. The Prophet had not made acquaintance with Scriptures of any religion, nor was he a member of any faith; nevertheless, he was a noble, honorable, beloved, trustworthy and truthful member of his society. In the history of the Arabs this was established and we still have the history.

Muhammed was asked by some young person, "Tell me something nobody else can tell me". I get that attitude, sometimes, from some persons. That is an attitude. "You are so special. You know so much. What I heard so far, I can get it from around the corner. I know where I can get that. I know some place to go and get that. So, I need you to tell me something that nobody else can tell me." The Prophet surprised him. He gave him a real, plain and simple reply. He said, "Say, 'I have believed!' And thereafter, be upright!" Here, he connected belief and faith with uprightness, didn't he? So, what is the real faith? The real faith is the faith that is established upon uprightness, or that blossoms upon uprightness. He said, "Say, 'I have accepted faith. I have believed'; thereafter, be upright."

Nature and Character of Islamic Democracy Forgotten

Now, to compare American democracy with Islamic democracy we must understand that Prophet Muhammed is a leader who invited the opinions of his people, his followers in certain matters, or when facing certain situations. But where were their opinions based that he asked for? He asked for their opinions, but their opinions had to be based on what was revealed, the Word of G_d, the Qur'an. Regrettably, sometimes, the nature and character of an Islamic democracy is forgotten.

The nature and character of an Islamic democracy, in some ways, is different from the nature and character of American democracy. For example, we are not at liberty in Islam to come up with our own opinions unless our opinions are founded on the Qur'an (the Word of G_d) and the sunnah (practices) of Prophet Muhammed. Being that the community of people that he was leading was newly invited to the religion themselves, many times, their own wishes were at odds with Allah's Intent, and Allah's Purpose. So, the Prophet received guidance from G_d and the guidance said, *"If you were to obey them in much of what they are requesting, you would, certainly, fall into misfortune "*; "You", meaning the Prophet.[53]

So, we have to be aware of that. If we would follow the notions and the ideas that people suggest among us, we would go off track. We have to follow only those proposals, notions, or suggestions, that require that we find proof and support in the Qur'an and in the practices (sunnah) of the Prophet. If we can't find support for what they ask of us, or offer us in the Qur'an, or the practices of the Prophet, we don't follow it. We reject it on the basis of the Qur'an and the hadith (authentic reports) and sunnah of the Prophet. And we have to, also, be aware that the devil, he is more cunning than the people. The devil is much wiser, more cunning, than the people. The devil will overtax you with things that Allah (G_d) has established.

Beware of Proposals That Overtax Us

Therefore, beware of the devil who will propose a good thing that is established in the Qur'an and that is established in the sunnah, but it will be overtaxing us. For example, the devil may say, "Well, wait a minute. Before you act upon what the Imam has said, let us check the Qur'an and the sunnah". If you have to stop at every minute, or every time that I say something and search the Qur'an and search the sunnah, you should say, "Wait a minute, now. We will check it out later, if it is necessary. He is in that position because we trust him. If we run into difficulty, then we will check him out".

Beware of the devil. The devil is one who will come among us and say, "How many times does the imam have you all praying? How many rakats (steps in the prayer) are you doing? Oh no, you should do sixteen rakats!" He wants to overtax us. If he can't convert you to his way, then he wants to make your way burdensome and miserable.

Language of the Constitution of the United States

Now, let us look at life, liberty and the pursuit of happiness; the language of the Constitution of the United States. Listen now, "Life" and "Liberty". You not only have the right to have your life, but you have the right to have your life free to be educated and to get the benefits that all other citizens get in the society, or in the nation. That's what it's saying. The interpretation is the right to have property. Life, liberty and the pursuit of happiness, the interpretation is the right to have property; and we know a man without the ownership of anything can't be happy; not if he's a true man. How can you be happy and you own nothing? You don't own your own clothes. You don't own your own house. You don't own your own animal to ride on, or a horse to ride around on. You don't own your own tools to work with. You own nothing. You don't even own yourself. How can you be happy?

Before Any Nation Known Man Was Free to Own Land

This is talking about something that is above tools. When it says, "The right to own property", that means land, to have some land of your own to do what you want with it; to develop it; crops, minerals, forestry, whatever; the right to develop it; housing projects, whatever. That is what the Founding Fathers said that we have that right given to us by our G_d, that no nation gave us that right. Isn't that a fact of history? They were studying history, too. Before any nation was known man was free to own land and to work land, live off of the land; and to do whatever he could to develop that land; before any modern civilization, or nations were known.

So, they are basing this principle upon the reality that G_d made people like that and they had this before we formed these governments; and these governments have no right to take that away. Every man and woman are born to have this freedom, this liberty, this life and this right to own land and have property. But obviously, they lost that, didn't they? This came late in the history of the Christian Church so, obviously, they never saw it, or they lost it.

And as I said, it was Muhammed, the Prophet, the great, universal teacher, the mercy to all people, all nations, all worlds; it was Muhammed, the Prophet, his life and his works with the Qur'an, the Word of G_d, the last revelation, that awakened this, again, in the hearts and intellects of the best of the people. Because of that Martin Luther was able to see the backwardness of church society and their leaders and opened the door to light so that church leaders and the church society came out of darkness, ignorance and slavery into freedom, the sciences, and democracy; yes, democracy.

No Democracy for the Christian World Before Islam

There was no democracy for the Christian world before Islam. Kingdoms, dictators, rulers, the best of them saw the common person as an image of a human, but in reality, an animal; not a human being. That is what justified them not giving public education, not educating the common people. The common person had no right to be educated before Islam came to be practiced by Muhammed and his followers. There was no educating the common people and the women were not given equal respect before the courts with the men. They didn't do that. All of that came with Islam.

Consequently, don't think when Allah says of Muhammed in the Qur'an that, *"He is a mercy to all the worlds"*, that that's in your estimation: "Oh yes, Muhammed is a mercy to all the worlds!" This religion is beautiful. It is merciful! Muhammed, the Prophet, is a mercy to everybody. You have to know the condition that the world was in and you have to know how the presence of Islam taught by the first teacher, Muhammed, affected this world to make it change and to get better. You have to know how it awakened the human intellect to appreciate the universe as the place for exploration, for human discoveries and studies.[54]

Wake Up to Your Great Responsibility

It was the Qur'an that said, *"Travel throughout the world and see how G_d repeats creation".*[55] So, "Study old, ancient, creation and see how He repeated civilization, or creation". It was that message from Islam that reached them to make them want to go and start research, search the world, search history, dig in the earth to see if they could find signs of nations that existed that were buried before. It was because the Qur'an said, "There were others greater than you and they lost. They tumbled down. They disappeared as though they never existed here before". It told them to go out and search for it, travel. Al-Islam is the one that signaled the intellect to get back into its intellectual life.[56]

The brain was made to have a brain life, an intellectual life. It was dead and it was Islam and the leader, Muhammed, that signaled the brain and the human intellect to, "Wake up to your great responsibility that G_d created you for! And carry out your responsibility, so that you can have a beautiful, productive life"! Islam did that. G_d did that, when He revealed the Qur'an to Muhammed.

Prophet Muhammed Is Leader of the Modern World

So, I go back to what I said. We can prove it and there are some other scholars, I know, in the Islamic world that take this position and they are beautiful people. We could get on television and we could challenge anybody and prove that we are speaking the truth, according to history, that Muhammed is the leader of the modern world; not the Founding Fathers. He leads them! Prophet Muhammed leads the Founding Fathers. Prophet Muhammed is leading the leaders of the United States, right now. They can't find a better man. His logic, finally, gradually, as time passes, is the logic that's being accepted by the modern world leaders. And the United States is in the forefront following the great logic of the great, universal leader, Muhammed, the Prophet. Oh, that's too much to talk about! We would be all day and night talking about that, because there is so much in history that I can show you that if they had followed Muhammed's logic, they could have saved a lot of suffering, a lot of embarrassment to the nations.

No Civil War If Muhammed's Logic Had Been Followed

I have to tell you this. If they had followed Muhammed's logic to establish better conditions for African Americans as slaves, they could have avoided a civil war. Racism wouldn't have had to be created. Racism wouldn't have had an opportunity to present itself, if they had studied him carefully and followed Muhammed's logic for civilization, for nations; for rulers, for people, etc. I know this and I guarantee you they know it now. They didn't know it before, but they know it now.

A writer (Michael H. Hart) wrote a book on men who made the greatest contributions in the history of the world and out of all of them, Moses and Jesus Christ included, peace be upon them, he picked Muhammed, the Prophet, peace be upon him. He's not a Muslim but he picked Muhammed, the Prophet, based on the truth of history. He based his position upon the truth of history. There wasn't any guess work. He based his choice upon history that no man, no other human being ever achieved, in such a short span of time, what that man (Muhammed, the Prophet) achieved.[57] Now, Mr. Hart couldn't tell it all, because he would have shaken up the order of the world, if he had told it all. He didn't want to do that. But I'm sure he wanted them to say, "Hey, we are ignorant and working against our own selves, if we don't recognize this man, Muhammed!"

And I believe he had in his heart hope that great leaders among them would study Muhammed, the Prophet, after his book; would study him, again, look at him, again; study him, again to see what else he has done and what else he offers the world; what else has Muhammed, the Prophet, done for the world and what else does he offer the world; not of himself. Anything that you know of Prophet Muhammed is only because of the revelation of G_d to him; because Muhammed, himself, was unlearned. He was not the son of a learned people. He was not the son of scholars, or teachers. He had no friends who were such men, i.e., scholars, and teachers. He was not privy to any help from the great learned minds, no rabbi, nobody. That's in fulfillment of Scripture and Jesus is a sign of it.

Individual Thinking Influenced by Satan

You know, it seems that Satan can influence things on his own. Whenever he wants, he can bring the whole world under his influence. Why? It is because your individual thinking has been influenced by Satan. What the people have established is approved by Satan. As a result, we have democracy, but look at this democracy. It is represented by two parties, one democrat, the other republican; and you don't get the whole truth from either, do you? You get what each one gives you as a focus, focusing your attention on what they want to put your attention on.

So, the democrats focus your attention on what they want you to see and do. The republicans focus your attention on what they want you to see and do. Hence, these are two different parties, or two different perceptions of what is best for the citizens of America. They are not always disagreeing with each other, but they are always trying to get their bosses in position. Really, any two presidential candidates, representing the democrats and the republicans in today's world, are really in a very difficult situation, now, because the realities of the world are dictating that they both do the same thing. Therefore, they have to pretend they have differences. Subsequently, here is one harping on one issue and the other a different one. One is fighting with the war and the terrorists: "What are you going to do about terrorism?" And the other one is trying to appeal to the little man and says: "Look at what this guy is doing with your benefits. Look at how he is cutting you out of everything!"

Where is the ideology? This isn't ideology. They're not dealing with ideology. This is no conflict of ideologies, is it? No, it is a conflict of interest. The democrats say, "We have an interest in you and your life, the little man". The republicans are saying, "I can't tell you that I have an interest in my wealthy associates, so, I have to frighten you with this terrorism". That is scary! As a result, a lot of people are going to vote just because they are afraid the terrorists might get them. They might wake up and see a terrorist sitting on their couch, or something.

Hope for People All Around the World

In reality, we don't need a lot of people. I only need a few people to follow what G_d has given me. That's all I need. I don't need a lot of people. Eventually, after I'm dead, we will have success. It doesn't have to come, now. It can come long after I'm dead. Eventually, we'll have a new African American people and they'll be equipped, qualified, enlightened to protect their families for generations to come; to keep their families in the right light, on the right path for generations to come. Eventually, our successful living will attract more and more of the lost. We want the lost African Americans to come to us, so they can have life. That is going to happen, whether we do it, or not, because Allah is going to have somebody do it.

I don't see anything more important than that for me. Nothing is happening on this earth, for me, more important than that, because, ultimately, it will give hope to people all around the world, and shouldn't they come? The whole world, saw, witnessed us put down as black slaves, inferior and helpless, under white supremacy. Is it something that is hard for you to believe, that the G_d Who saw that happen, now, wants to lift some of us up so the whole world will see us and know that He has lifted us and compensated us for our losses that we suffered under the nations of the world?

What nation is innocent, when it comes to us (African Americans)? Not a one! There is not a single nation you can point to and say, "They are innocent". They were all mum, saying nothing while that (chattel slavery in America) was going on. That wasn't a big deal for them! It didn't bother them that much! You didn't hear of nations crying out, "Look at what America is doing to those human beings!" G_d cannot really compensate us, justly, by just making us the same with everybody else, like a lot of African Americans want saying, "We just want to be just like everybody else!" Well, they don't belong here with us.

A True Democracy That Can Live

To be clear, this is all religious talk. My criticism of what is going on downstairs, here on earth, is my criticism of Satan's plan against the natural man in his life that G_d wants to establish him upon that will enable us to have a true democracy that can live. "We hold these truths to be self-evident that all men are created equal and are endowed by their Creator". Isn't that the natural life that G_d gave us? "With certain unalienable rights, among these rights are life liberty and the pursuit of happiness." That is the powerful ideology that made possible the forming of this great government that makes every citizen, every man and woman that will be loyal to this government and faithful to the preservation of these United States, comfortable that, "I'm doing it for myself. This Constitution was written for me"! And that is true.

Selfishness Promotes Death of Rational Life

We have come to understand that selfish promotion of one's own interest invites, not only moral death, but the death of rational life, as well. To work against moral life is stupid, not wisdom. Wisdom is not to see moral life separate from rational life. We all, in these great heavenly religions as we, sometimes, call them, Judaism, Christianity and Islam, understand the fall of man, the fall of our father, Adam. It came only when he ate of a certain forbidden food and caused the generations to separate moral life from rational life, or to see them separately. Moral life will soon disappoint us, if it separates from rational life and rational life will soon disappoint us, if it separates from moral thought, or moral life. I believe that Islam and Christianity are the same in that we want to keep this life consistent, healthy and whole, or complete.

Christianity and Islam Separated by Political Interests

Muhammed, the Prophet, he said, "There will come a time when Jesus Christ and himself will be seen together"; peace and blessings be upon them both. We believe in the birth of Jesus Christ without the help of man, or without the involvement of a male; a man. Perhaps, I cannot use the same language, "The Immaculate Conception". I feel comfortable in my own self, but I do not feel that comfortable speaking as a student of Islamic knowledge, saying it, or putting it that way. That is why I have not put it that way. But I do feel comfortable, in my soul, with that language. Islam and Christianity are separated not by knowledgeable people in these two religions. They are separated by people who have political interests.

Lady Chiara Lubich and the Focolare Movement

We have the Focolore, an international movement of Catholics, founded by Lady Chiara Lubich who was experiencing as a child, as a young lady, a teenager about seventeen in Trent, Italy, the horrors of World War II; with bombs falling all around. Consequently, she decided to give her mind to Jesus Christ, peace be on him, as a servant, as a Catholic; as a person working hard to bring people to love one another, to call people back to Christ's love. I became acquainted with her reading her book on her life and I fell in love with her soul and her mind. Subsequently, we formed a friendship and that friendship now is a friendship for myself and those who are associated with me in the following and herself and those associated with her in her following around the world.[58]

The point I want to make here is that we need to study these two religions (Christianity and Islam) with innocent hearts. As it says in our book, the Qur'an: *"None can touch it"*, none can grasp the beauty and substance of the Qur'an, *"except the purified ones"*.[59] When we are innocent in our hearts and minds and in our souls, we do not have any intentions that will shame us before G_d, or the public. If we would disclose those intentions, it would show that we have transparency and G_d will guide us to the substance and purity of our Scriptures.

I have read the Bible very carefully and very diligently. First, I said to myself, "I want to be fair. I do not want to read the Bible and pick it apart and question everything. I want to be able to go through the book like I want to. I vow that I will not stop to take anything apart, or to question anything. I will read the Bible from cover to cover". I did that. G_d helped me to do that. At the same time, when I was making the pledge to myself to do it that way I, also, said, "And when I finish reading it that way, I'm going to pick it apart." And I did. However, the first reading converted me to the purity of the Bible. I saw a continuous line of purity, from Genesis to Revelation. So, G_d put me in a situation where I could study it and look at it, critically and I did. So, I came to conclusion that our religions want a world order that respects G_d and has man (the human being) working in the service of mankind under G_d. G_d says He does not want anything from us. He needs nothing from us. He only wants, from us, our obedience.

Time for the World to Address the Loss of Morals in Society

In Islam, emphasis on behavior is very strong. Muslims are not to behave any kind of way. We can't follow the world of cultural trends that takes us from life to death, back to life and then to death. To me, nations that permit that kind of cultural life to control the lives of the masses of people and the leaders will, also, fall victim to it; because the common denominator for all of us is our moral life, our sensitive souls that G_d gave us; our emotions, etc. And no one is safe no matter how educated we become.

No matter how powerful we become, no one is safe from the danger of losing this sensitive soul if we allow the influences that are against the health of the soul to take over the life of the public, or the life of society. In my opinion, we are no better than those ancient nations who regulated their societies by that kind of logic, or that kind of insight into the nature of human behavior. I believe that it is time for this great world that has advanced us in science and technology, and also, in human nature, to address the loss of morals in society. We have become more socially mature because of the great advances we have made in the sciences and with our particular experiences that we have with our democracy in the United States of America. So, my prayer is that we study the society, study what governs our society, and get the devil out of our society.

Healing Is Going to Come

Today, we find the old sins that are written in the Bible have grown so big and have become so prevalent and so common that the legislators want to legislate rights for them. We are at a point where those people who used to be a threat to the decent order of man's life on this earth are recognized and given the same rights that the decent people have. Now, you know, that is something that shows you that Satan has really taken over, hasn't he? Satan has gotten into power with the wicked people. He has multiplied his crowd. He has increased his crowd to such numbers, now, that he can use democracy and make it work for him. Isn't that something?

We are living in the end of time, the Day of Judgment, the Great Day of Religion. I am as convinced of that as I am convinced of anything real in my life; that that time that was predicted, prophesized, we are living in it, right now. It is not going to come, it is here! And thank G_d (Allah), we are situated to see it end! We are situated to live long enough to see the beast die and all of his filth die with him! It is coming! That is here, too! When a disease reaches its fullness, its terminal, end state, it looks the worst. But that's the sign that it won't be going any further. It won't be increasing, anymore. Healing is going to come, now, for those who kept life. As for the others, they are dead. You can't do anything for them. But those who held their life in the terminal state, we expect healing to come and that's where we are.

We are at the point where the corruption that Satan encouraged for man on this earth has reached its terminal state and now, the process of purifying has begun. And look at how strong Allah has made some of these religious bodies on this earth. They are Jews, Christians, Buddhists, Muslims and others. They all are coming together to address the protection of the family life and to address the need to fight immorality and corruption in the society; and they are doing a beautiful job. I know this because I have interacted with some of them by me belonging to some world organizations, like the organization, Religions for Peace.

Greatest Impediment to Harmony and Peace in the World

The greatest impediment I see to a possibility for harmony and peace in the world, today, is world powers imposing what they believe is good for the world on others. For example, there are some hardcore Zionists in Israel and they will not even let the Israeli public, the citizens of Israel, have a free voice. They work with whoever will work with them around the world and they are trying to impose what they believe should be the order for mankind on this planet. We differ with that and I think that is the greatest impediment to peace. I wish our country would not be so loyal to the wrong people and to a small group of people while disrespecting what the world wants. We should not impose our democracy on anybody. We should invite people to copy the best that we have, if they choose to. But we should not impose it upon them. We should let them work out their own future and have their own form of government.

Justice Even More Important Than American Democracy

As I said, I believe we are living in the end of time, the Day of Judgment, the time for the conclusion of the great issues of prophecy, or Scripture. Never before have human beings on this planet earth, been connected all around the world and we're being connected in the most serious ways. We are being connected economically and, therefore, we have to be connected politically. Time is gone for one nation to be operating independently. No, it has to operate in concert with other world leaders and other societies around the world. There has to be agreement. There has to be acceptance, inclusion and recognition of the rights of others, their political rights, etc., just as you recognize your own rights. Our governmental leaders have been trying to give the world democracy and no one nation should give other nations its plan, its political idea. All of us should be free. All nations should be free to choose for themselves what will be their political idea. We should want justice. It is more important than even American democracy and the time is here for that.

The Greatest Hope Is with the People Who Are in Heaven

Consequently, the greatest hope I see is with the people who are in heaven. There are people in heaven. They are not angels. They are human, too, in heaven; and they are the best of our moral leaders who want an ethical world. They want to have all nations respected and treated fairly and they want to have people free to choose their own community life, their own way of life. That is the hope. So, while we are seeing the dupes of Satan working hard and having their heyday, we, also, see a strong effort in the heavens and healing is beginning to grow in the earth. The point I am trying to make, here, is don't be down-hearted and don't lose faith now! Live your faith, consciously!

Religion to be Practiced Consciously

To my fellow Muslims living in this democratic society called, the United States of America, I say again, as I said earlier, "Don't live your Islamic life unconsciously! Islamic life is to be lived consciously. It is not a life of faith, only. It is after the order of Ibraheem (Abraham), the man who couldn't be satisfied with something his intelligence didn't agree with. He had to have a religion that he practiced consciously, and it had to respect his intelligence".

That is why it says in the Qur'an that this is, *"The millah (order) of Ibraheem (Abraham), the sane in faith"*. (Q.3.95) The Qur'anic

Arabic word, "Millah", doesn't actually mean, "an order". It means a hope, but a hope that has been followed; or a hope that has been living through generations going back to Adam. It is the hope that G_d created when He created the human soul.

Hope Is Already There in the Soul

That hope was in the human soul from the beginning. G_d created the human soul to know, to understand, to want good, to want progress for a good life. All that is in the soul by way of our creation and it only needs the objective world to awaken it. Once we face the objective world, then the soul starts expressing itself through our conscious and through our intelligence. But that is already there in the soul. You come with that. It is in the nature of every human person.

So, glory is just a step away! Praise be to Allah (G_d)! This is an ugly and a dreadful time and at the same time it is a great time that will bring rejoicing to the innocent souls that stay with G_d. It is coming very soon! May G_d's Peace and Blessing be with you!

NOTES

All Qur'an references are from the Abdullah Yusuf Ali translation of the original Arabic into English. All Bible references are from the King James version.

Preface and Introduction

[1] *The Peculiar Institution: Slavery in the Ante-Bellum South*, Stampp, Kenneth M., p. 3.

[2] *Democracy in America and Two Essays on America*, De Tocqueville, Alexis, pp. 371-2.

[3] Q.73.15.

[4] N.T., Matt.6.10; Luke.11.2.

[5] Q.2.193.

[6] Q.31.13.

[7] O.T., Exod.3.14; N.T., 1 Corin.15.10.

[8] Q.96.1-2.

[9] Q.17.70.

[10] Q.17.15.

1

Strengthening Our American Citizenship

[11] Q.2.3.

[12] Q.5.116

[13] Q.96.1-5.

[14] Q.3.96

[15] Q.18:110, 41:6.

[16] N.T., Prov. 23:7

[17] Q.95.1-4.

[18] 4:76

2

Coming to the Qibla of the Muslims

[19] O.T., Amos.8.11.

[20] Q.2.285.

[21] Q.2.30.

[22] Q.3.110.

[23] Q.2.144.

[24] Q.6.38.

[25] See, Spellberg, Denise, *Thomas Jefferson's Qur'an: Islam and the Founders,* Random House LLC, New York, NY, 2013.

3

Sharing America's Freedom Space

[26] The Hijra is the name given to the event when Muhammed, the Prophet, and his followers emigrated from Mecca to Medina.

[27] "Friends, Romans, countrymen, lend me your ears", words spoken by Marc Antony, in the *Tragedy of Julius Caesar,* a play and tragedy by William Shakespeare first performed in 1599.

[28] Khan, 'Abdul Waheed, *The Personality of Allah's Last Messenger*, pp. 58-62, International Islamic Publishing House, Saudi Arabia (1420 AH/1999 CE).

[29] On February 26, 1975, Imam W. Deen Mohammed, was elected the leader of the Nation of Islam, succeeding his father, Elijah Mohammed who had led the community since 1933.

[30] Q.10.16.

[31] Q.18.110; 41.6.

[32] Q.42.38.

[33] Q.31.28; 67.2.

[34] O.T., Malachi.4.6.

4

Consultation and Consensus in Islam

35 Q.55.15.

36 And [it is reported] in al-Tirmidhi from Ibn 'Abbas, he said: The Messenger of Allah (Allah bless him and grant him peace) said: "The hand of Allah is with the Jama'ah." [It is] an uncommon hadith. And [he narrated] the like of it from Ibn 'Umar, he said: The Messenger of Allah (Allah bless him and grant him peace) said: "Verily Allah will not unite my ummah" – or he said, "the ummah of Muhammad"– "on misguidance, and the hand of Allah is with the Jama'ah, and whoever is isolated, is isolated in the Fire."[

37 Q.42.38.

38 Q.58:1.

39 Q.35.6; 36.60

40 N.T., Rev.5.6.

41 Q.17.70.

5

Islam and American Democracy

[42] ʿĀd was an ancient tribe mentioned frequently in the Qurʾan. ʿĀd is usually placed in Southern Arabia, in a location referred to as al-ʾAḥqāf. The tribe's members, referred to as ʿĀdites, formed a prosperous nation, until they were destroyed in a violent storm. According to Islamic tradition, the storm came after they had rejected the teachings of the Prophet, Hud.

[43] Q.16.125.

[44] "What, to the American slave, is your 4th of July? I answer; a day that reveals to him, more than all other days in the year, the gross injustice and cruelty to which he is the constant victim. To him, your celebration is a sham; your boasted liberty, an unholy license; your national greatness, swelling vanity; your sounds of rejoicing are empty and heartless; your denunciation of tyrants, brass fronted impudence; your shouts of liberty and equality, hollow mockery; your prayers and hymns, your sermons and thanksgivings, with all your religious parade and solemnity, are, to Him, mere bombast, fraud, deception, impiety, and hypocrisy -- a thin veil to cover up crimes which would disgrace a nation of savages. There is not a nation on the earth guilty of practices more shocking and bloody than are the people of the United States, at this very hour." Phillips, Foner, *"The Meaning of July Fourth for the Negro", The Life and*

Writings of Frederick Douglass, Volume II Pre-Civil War Decade 1850-1860, International Publishers Co., Inc., New York, 1950.

[45] Q.52.48.

[46] Al-Fatiha, Q.1.1-7.

[47] *"The praise is for G_d, the Lord of all the worlds (all systems of knowledge)".* Q.1.2.

[48] See the opening chapter (surah) of the Qur'an, Al-Fatiha.

[49] Sura (chapter) 90 of the Qur'an.

[50] Q.90.2, "Al-Balad", or "The City", commentary #6131.

[51] N.T., John.3.13.

[52] Q.26.78.

[53] Q.49:7

[54] Q.21.107: *"We sent thee not, but as a mercy for all creatures".*

[55] Q.10.34; 27.64; 29.19; 30.11; 30.27.

[56] Q.22.45-6.

[57] Hart, Michael H., *The 100: A Ranking of the Most Influential Persons in History,* Citadel Press (Kensington Publishing Corp.), New York, NY, 1992.

[58] Lubich, Chiara, *May They All Be One: Origins and Life of the Focolare Movement,* New City Press, Hyde Park, NY, 1968.

[59] Q.56.79.

Glossary of Terms

Allah. The One and Only G_d.

Ayat (plural, Ayaat). Qur'anic Arabic word meaning, "a sign"; a verse in the Qur'an.

W. Fard Muhammad (aka W. D. Fard, Wallace D. Muhammad). The founder of the Lost Found Nation of Islam in the Wilderness of North America (Nation of Islam); the teacher of the Honorable Elijah Mohammed.

Al-Fatiha. The opening chapter of the Holy Qur'an.

Adhan. The call to prayer, using the human voice, in the Islamic faith.

Bil Ghaib. The Unseen.

Focolare. An international organization that promotes the ideals of unity and universal brotherhood. The word, "Focolare", is Italian for, "Hearth of the fireplace", expressing the organization's ideal of promoting warm human sentiments and love. Its official name is, "The Work of Mary". The movement began in Trent, Italy, during World War II, among a small group of Catholic girls, meticulously studying the New Testament, as they huddled in shelters, waiting for the bombs to stop falling, with Chiara Lubich, as their leader. Chiara, with her G_d-inspired, "Charism, or, "spirituality of unity", led the group to become an international movement, promoting oneness and unity among all people of faith, all human beings, until her passing, in 2008. Today, the International Focolare Movement operates in more than 182 countries and includes members from a plethora of religious traditions.

G_d. In order to show due reverence to the name of G_d Almighty, we do not use a spelling that can, in the reverse, spell, "dog".

Hadith. The collection of the reported sayings of Muhammed, the Prophet.

Haneef (plural, Hunafaa). A human being, upright in his nature, never bowing down to anything in creation; a person who has uprightness in him. In Scripture, Abraham (Ibraheem) is seen as the first person who is haneef.

Hijra (Hijrah), the Islamic New Year. Marks the event, in 622 CE, when Muhammed, the Prophet, emigrated from Mecca to Medina and set up the first Islamic ummah (community, or state). The Islamic calendar dates from the Hijra, which is why Islamic dates have the suffix A.H, instead of CE.

Honorable Elijah Mohammed. The leader of the Lost Found Nation of Islam in the Wilderness of North America (The Nation of Islam) from 1933-1975; the father of Imam W. Deen Mohammed.

Imam. In Islam, the person that goes out front to lead the group prayer.

Islam. More properly given as, Al-Islam, in the Qur'an. It is the last of the three monotheistic religions (after Judaism and Christianity). It was established by the revelation of the Qur'an to Muhammed, the Prophet, a little more than 600 years after the time of Jesus Christ.

Jahiliyyah. The age of ignorance. The name given to the period of darkness and ignorance in Arabia before the Qur'an was revealed to Muhammed, the Prophet.

Jihad. Striving, struggling, or fighting in the way of G_d.

Ka'bah. The house built by Ibraheem (Abraham) and his son, Isma'il (Ishmael), that is the orientation for the Muslim prayer performed five times a day.

Kafir. A rejecter of faith in Allah (G_d) and truth for mankind. In the revelation of the Qur'an, Satan (Shaitan) is identified as the first kafir.

Khalifah. A name, or title, given by Allah, in the revelation of Qur'an, referring to a coming, "successor", or "ruler", He is making in the earth that is not to be an individual, but a social order, a governmental order, that will be entrusted to rule, supported by human intelligence, human excellence, and human decency; a divinely-inspired republic.

Minaret. A tower, that is usually part of a mosque, with a balcony from which a mu'adhdhin calls Muslims to prayer.

Mu'adhdhin. The Muslim official of a mosque (masjid) who calls the faithful to prayer five times a day, using the human voice. The first mu'adhdhin in Islamic history was Bilal Ibn Rabah.

Muhammed, the Prophet. The last Prophet of Scripture who received the holy Scripture for Muslims, the Qur'an, over 23 years that established the religion of Islam and the model Islamic community.

Nation of Islam. More properly, the Lost Found Nation of Islam in the Wilderness of North America; the proto-Islamic movement founded, circa 1930, in Detroit, Michigan, by Mr. W. Fard Muhammad and was led by the Honorable Elijah Mohammed from 1933-1975.

Qibla. The direction (towards the Ka'bah in Mecca) that the Muslim orientates himself/herself towards in order to perform salat (prayer) five times a day.

Qur'an (Koran). The Word of G_d revealed to Muhammed, the Prophet, over a period of 23 years. It is the number one source of guidance for Muslims.

Shuraa Baynahum. Literally, "Consultation with each other"; the foundation of Islamic democracy.

Salat. The formal prayer ritual, in Islam. Salat requires the adherent to pray (in a group) five times a day at prescribed times.

Shahadah. The declaration of faith in Islam. This declaration of faith is completed by saying, "Ash-shadu anla ilaaha illallah, wa ash-shadu anna Muhammedar Rasulullah. I declare (witness) that there is no deity, nothing to worship, to pray to as a god, except the One G_d; and I declare (witness) that Muhammed is the Messenger of G_d."

Shaitan, Shaytan. The Qur'anic Arabic word for Satan, or the devil.

Sunnah. The lifestyle, i.e., sayings and traditions, of Muhammed, the Prophet; the number two source of guidance for Muslims.

Ulema. A body of Muslim scholars recognized as having special knowledge of Islamic sacred law and theology; an Islamic council of learned men.